Praise for *Just Love* by Jayne Ozanne

'A heartfelt plea for love in all its glory, from a brave woman on her journey from despair to hope. Jayne's story is proof that sometimes the hardest paths can lead to wonderful places.' **Caroline Wyatt, broadcaster**

'This is not a comfortable book. It is Jayne's personal struggle to be true to herself and to God. Indeed you cannot be true to God if you cannot be true to and about yourself. It is also her search for love – spiritual, emotional and physical. Jayne bares her soul in pursuit of a more just and honest world – and Church.' **The Rt Revd James Jones KBE, formerly Bishop of Liverpool**

'*Just Love* is a compelling story. But it's not just Jayne's story; it is a call to a journey for the entire Church as we respond to Jayne's love for God and passion to serve the Church. Whatever your views on human sexuality, it is a journey we must all take together.' **Joel Edwards, international speaker, writer and broadcaster, and former director of the Evangelical Alliance UK**

'Powerful, poignant and prophetic – Jayne Ozanne's vivid autobiography testifies to a remarkable and resilient person, who has walked an uneasy path, fraught with darkness and difficulties. Yet what comes through, time and again, is a courageous mind and faith-filled life that is determined not to be overcome. Jayne's prescient work – creative, challenging and campaigning – is truly inspiring. Spiritually wise and theologically acute, this book challenges us with its freshness and frankness. Her work in the church as both a leader and dissenting voice stand as an important sign for the times: a sentinel that calls on those who hold authority and wield power to act with greater compassion and courage. This extraordinary autobiography will inspire many, convict some, rouse others – and should concern us all.' **The Very Revd Professor Martyn Percy, Dean of Christ Church, Oxford**

'Gripping, moving, searing, honest: a manifesto for living life and love to the full.' **Ysenda Maxtone Graham, critic for *The Times***

'A deeply personal account, not just of an individual exploring her emerging sexuality but also of the workings of the little-understood charismatic evangelical wing of the established church in the latter part of the 20th century. I've always admired Jayne's immense courage, energy and capacity for forgiveness, and never more so than now. This story of the changes she is helping bring about is only the beginning. It is essential reading for anyone seeking insight into the complex morality of the Church today.' **Ruth Gledhill, Multimedia Editor, *The Tablet* and editorial advisor, *Christian Today***

'This is Jayne's personal story of how, as an evangelical Christian, she was consumed by self-hate and internalised homophobia. It almost crushed her. But after much angst, she eventually made the leap to self-acceptance and LGBT+ advocacy within the Church. It is a reminder of the harm that is caused when religion puts dogma before love, and of the power of love to challenge injustice.' **Peter Tatchell, Peter Tatchell Foundation**

'Jayne Ozanne's book describes the life of a person of faith who has lived true to her faith. Jayne combines intellectual prowess with a talent for truth-telling and has walked the corridors of power in the Church and in the corporate worlds. She documents her struggle to accept her own sexual identity. For years she followed bad advice from good people and endured years of misery and inner turmoil. Finally able to trust her own prayer, she has enjoyed a loving relationship with a woman.' **The Revd Canon Mpho Tutu van Furth, ordained Episcopal priest, and executive director of the Desmond and Leah Tutu Legacy Foundation**

'Jayne is a woman of compassion and strength. She has contributed richly to the life of the world and of the Church – as you read this book you'll see how. She has the courage of a difference-maker, and the focus and devotion of a woman of faith who loves God and who wants to see justice done. And she believes that all the people God made – all the people God loves – are worth fighting for.' **The Rt Revd Paul Bayes, Bishop of Liverpool**

'Some books have to be written; some stories have to be told, and this is one of them. *Just Love* is a deeply moving, honest and personal account of the pain and harsh reality of what it too often means to be gay within the world of the Church today. But, even more than that, it is, at the same time, a profoundly life-affirming and hope-filled memoir for all those who find themselves travelling the same road.' **The Revd Steve Chalke, Baptist minister, and founder of the Oasis Charitable Trust**

'What do you do if your evangelical faith and your identity are in conflict? Jayne Ozanne writes of her experiences of conversion, breakdown and self-discovery in this deeply personal and at times shocking account. She challenges people of all persuasions to put God's love above all and follow where it leads, whatever the cost. This is a compelling and ultimately hopeful story.' **The Very Revd Dr David Ison, Dean of St Paul's Cathedral**

'This autobiography gives a startling insight into a world of evangelical faith where direct messages from God, prophecies, healings and demonic oppressions are the stuff of everyday experience. Jayne Ozanne was welcomed as a representative of such a faith into the highest councils of Church and State, while she also held a series of senior jobs in industry and international relations. The central drama is the torturing disjunction between official religious affiliation and the interior reality of loneliness and yearning for a partner of the same sex. It is hard not to agree with her psychiatrist who early on advised Jayne to change her religion.

'But the glory of this tale is that she did not. She stayed true to her conviction that faith and gayness are both gifts of the God who is Love. Her story is an inspiration to anyone struggling with the same issues today.' **The Very Revd Dr Jeffrey John, Dean of St Albans Cathedral**

'Beautifully written; compelling to read; totally honest and vulnerable, yet told with good humour and grace. This deeply personal story ranks alongside the truly great biographies of famous missionaries past and present. It is hugely well worth reading for that aspect of the story alone, aside from Jayne's struggle with her sexuality; anyone who dismisses her story for that reason does so to their own great loss. Here is a woman who, from her childhood days of confessing Jesus Christ as her Saviour and Lord, has lived out her vocation with such integrity and faithfulness –

and has a truly astonishing catalogue of missionary adventures, worldwide to tell. But the aspect, weaved through her story, in which Jayne struggles to come to terms with her sexuality is a hugely important one. Even today, there are some Christians who will struggle with her conclusions, but if we are to believe the words of Jesus, "You will know them by their fruit", then after all she has achieved in Christ's name for so many people across the world, to dismiss this woman of God who has lived with such integrity, raises a very real question: "Who on earth remains that can be trusted?" Because as well as seeing what a Christian life and vocation, faithfully lived out, can look like, Jayne's remarkable and courageous story deserves to be heard by all, most especially those who thus far remain to be convinced – that you can be gay and Christian.' **Jeremy Marks, founder and director of the former ministry The Courage Trust**

'This book is as important as it is compelling. A beautifully-written reconciliation of faith and sexuality which moved me to tears. The powerful words gripped my heart and nourished my faith.' **Philip Baldwin, LGBT/HIV rights activist, Stonewall Role Model, and writer for *Gay Times* and *The Huffington Post***

'Jayne Ozanne's biography is a groundbreaking book that beautifully weaves her own personal journey towards reconciling her faith and sexuality and the radical Gospel imperative to "just love". Her story is one that will resonate with many LGBT+ Christians in every corner of the globe and provoke international conversation for years to come. This book is a gift, not just to the LGBT+ Christian community, but to the Church of Jesus Christ at large. Get ready to be challenged, convicted, and transformed.' **Brandan Robertson, Lead Pastor of Missiongathering Christian Church, San Diego, USA, writer and activist**

Just Love

First published in 2018 by
Darton, Longman and Todd Ltd
1 Spencer Court
140 – 142 Wandsworth High Street
London SW18 4JJ

Reprinted 2018

ISBN: 978-0-232-53375-0

Some names and identifying details have been changed to protect
the privacy of those involved.

Cover image (detail): 'By Your Side' (mixed media on paper) 2016, © Lucy Ash.
Cover photograph by Ben McDade Photography.

A catalogue record for this book is available from the British Library

Designed and produced by Judy Linard
Printed and bound in Great Britain by Short Run Press Ltd, Exeter.

Just Love

A journey of
self-acceptance

Jayne Ozanne

Jayne Ozanne (signature)

DARTON·LONGMAN + TODD

To My Parents,

who have been led by love on a journey of faith

to their own place of acceptance;

and for all those who bravely seek to travel the same path.

Know that God walks with you.

Contents

Foreword

I first came across Jayne Ozanne at General Synod in 2000. She was an imposing figure – an evangelical firebrand on Archbishops' Council. Initially appointed by the previous evangelical Archbishop of Canterbury, George Carey, she would then serve under Rowan Williams, whose liberal catholic spirituality alarmed some conservatives.

The five years which followed were to be a time of great change for many who struggled with sexuality, faith and Church. The election of Gene Robinson in the USA as the first openly gay Anglican bishop caused uproar in the world-wide Anglican Communion. Soon afterwards in England, Jeffrey John was appointed Bishop of Reading, and then forced to withdraw following a loud evangelical outcry. Many were caught up in the issues surrounding human sexuality like never before, including me.

But for Jayne, that struggle was not just a Church issue. It was an ever-present reality with which she had struggled her whole life, not in a cold, abstract vacuum, but in the very core of her being. What is more, it was a secret she had had to keep from the world at large.

If I had met Jayne ten years earlier, and if she had been able to talk openly with me about her sexuality, I would have advised her to follow the standard evangelical path – obedience to God's Word, prayer and perhaps healing, possibly even deliverance. I am grateful that we did not meet then, as I have already had to repent many times for the burdens I placed on LGBT+ people before God changed my heart and mind.

Our worlds almost collided in 2004 when General Synod

debated sexuality. In the same debate where Jayne wondered if she had the courage to 'come out', I was planning to come out in a different way, not as gay, but as something equally dangerous to conservative Christians – as a pro-gay evangelical.

In that debate Jayne was called to speak and you can find her speech in Chapter 9. I was not called and went home frustrated before turning my speech into a letter to the Church of England Newspaper. The response which came from its publication led to the formation of Accepting Evangelicals – the first evangelical, pro-gay campaigning group in the UK.

I remember listening to Jayne's speech at Synod and being surprised. Hearing her name called, I expected to hear sound evangelical doctrine, persuasively delivered. Instead I heard a pastoral call to consider those who are plunged into despair by our church rhetoric. I spoke to Jayne afterwards but did not guess that she was talking about herself.

It did not surprise me, however, when ten years later I saw Jayne sitting in a pew at a LGBT Christian celebration where I had been invited to preach. We talked together afterwards and her story came flooding out.

In this book you will read of Jayne's childhood, her impressive business career, and how God called her into the corridors of power on the Archbishops' Council and beyond. More importantly, you will also hear of the pain and struggle caused by the false dichotomy between faith and sexuality which she had been presented with. Jayne writes as she speaks, both forthright and at times brutally honest, but her message is love. JUST LOVE.

Jayne is not alone. Even today there are churches who delegitimise gay, lesbian and bi people, describing their sexuality as merely 'experiencing same-sex attraction'. By defining it in such superficial terms, they encourage others to believe that it can be changed by obedience, reparative therapy, healing or deliverance. Others talk about being gay as simply a 'lifestyle choice' which can be reversed by repentance and forgiveness.

Foreword

This book exposes the fallacy of such responses and the harm they cause.

I remember hearing John Bell from the Iona Community say, 'If being gay is so wrong, why does God keep making gay people?' Sexuality is an integral part of our created being, whether heterosexual or homosexual or somewhere in between.

The Revd Benny Hazlehurst
Founder member of Accepting Evangelicals

Prologue

Autumn 1997

I lay back in bed and looked up at the curtains. It was one of those perfect autumn days, with a piercing light that streamed through the chinks making patterns on the ceiling.

'Damn it, I'm still here!' was all I could think.

The moment is forever etched in my mind. The old faded curtains, given to me by a neighbour from home in Guernsey; the brightly coloured walls of my West London flat, boldly decorated by the previous owners, the now-famous Macdonald brothers; and the warm cocoon of my duvet.

I had gone to bed the previous night begging God to take me in my sleep. I'd had enough. I hadn't the strength to go on – the deep well of aloneness seemed so all-consuming. There was no way out, no way forward. All I could sense was an endless isolated nothingness filled with continual pain – and I just couldn't cope with that stress anymore. I wanted out – who wouldn't? But I knew I couldn't and wouldn't actually 'do' anything, so instead I just longed and prayed for it.

But here I was, much to my dismay – still alive, still breathing.

I watched the light continue to dance through the curtains, reflecting the movement of cars in the street below, and out of nowhere a thought came crashing into my mind: 'I feel like an animal'.

Earlier that year, following my admission to the Priory Hospital, I had watched the somewhat eccentric Mexican film *Like Water for Chocolate*. It had resonated with me on so many levels – an unrequited love story of pain and injustice. The scene I now pictured was of the heartbroken heroine, Tita, taking refuge in a dovecote and becoming just like the birds she was surrounded by.

'I feel like an animal!'

I felt a surge of anger course through me and shouted out aloud into the empty room: 'What makes me any different to an animal, heh, God?! I eat, I drink, I sleep, I go to the bathroom ...'

Tears of sheer frustration rolled down onto my pillow as I encountered deafening silence.

And then, a voice – so recognisable and so familiar, so quiet and yet so reassuring, that said: 'Your ability to love, Jayne.'

I thought about this briefly then, emboldened by my anger and the painful memory this had touched, I snapped back: 'No, I'm not having that. Harry loved me! Animals can love you know!'

Harry, my darling, beautiful six-month old kitten, who had snuggled up to me every night and suckled on my hair. Harry, that naughty, playful ball of life, who had kept me going through some of the most difficult days of my life. Harry, whose cries had torn my heart when I left him at the vet on my way into hospital. Harry, who had finally been the 'tipping point' for me as I realised that the one thing that had loved me was the one thing I had so deeply, even if unintentionally, hurt.

Animals can most definitely love.

'Ah, Jayne, but you can *respond* in love to *any* situation I put you in, because I AM love, and I AM in you, and you are in Me!'

Was it an audible voice? I still don't know. It was as loud and clear as someone standing right next to me. But whether real or imagined, this articulated truth turned my life upside down.

'I AM love.'

I finally understood. It was so simple but so profound.

Prologue

I could respond in love to any situation that I was in, because God IS love.

It really is just that simple.

We are called to JUST LOVE – no matter who, no matter where, no matter how, no matter why.

JUST LOVE! That's all.

The rest is up to God.

CHAPTER ONE

Guernsey Girl

Summer 1977

I first met Jesus on a beach. It was the perfect setting for a Guernsey girl – down on the sandy expanse that forms Rocquaine bay. As it happens, it was the place where we would spend most of our summer holidays, the nearest of the beaches to our home in the southern parish of Torteval on the small Channel Island of Guernsey.

Ozanne is a well-known Guernsey name – we go back generations, evidently. Once, while I was living in Paris, I set myself the task of finding the source of the river Ozanne, which I knew to be a tributary of the Loire. After hours of driving, I finally ended up in a little village – I still can't remember the name – where water seemed to 'bubble up' out of nowhere. I remember looking at all the road and house names and realising that many were ones I recognised – old Guernsey names that were associated with both my grandparents: Bisson and Priaulx. I therefore developed the romantic idea that my Guernsey forefathers had more than likely been refugees, fleeing some bloody Huguenot uprising or other. They had headed north to Sarnia, as the island is locally known, which has long provided a place of refuge – a neutral territory, as decreed by a papal bull in 1483. It is now a crown dependency. After all, aren't most of us refugees from somewhere?

Family tradition has it that Ozanne means 'forerunner' or 'heralder' – the person who went ahead of the founding fathers to prepare those in the villages to hear the Gospel. I must admit I loved this idea, and so wasn't that keen on adopting the more the official definition (according to Google) which says it is a French version of the Hebrew word for 'save now'. Whatever its true meaning, I remember being teased mercilessly at school whenever we sang 'Sing Hosanna', which always inevitably became 'Sing Ozanna'. Perhaps more annoying was the taunt 'Ozanna in the highest', said every Christmas, given the fact I was quite tall. For all that, though, I was always very proud of having such an unusual surname, with a strong Biblical meaning and heritage.

I'm also very proud of being a 'Guern', with full residency rights thanks to the fact I was schooled on the island. However, I probably need to own up to the fact that I was actually born in Barnstaple, Devon while my father was stationed at RAF Chivenor. He had been one of the RAF's top fighter pilots, having won the Queen's Medal at Cranwell, but had sadly had a nasty 'prang' that left him with severe burns and yet an undeterred courage to continue flying. As such, he flew a range of fighter jets at a time when science was still trying to understand how best to counter the significant G force that he and others were having to pull. He had met my mother – an air hostess, whose father was teaching mathematics at RAF Cranwell – on a blind date set up by the Airforce Chaplain, Uncle David (as he was affectionately known), in 1966. They married in 1967 and I was born in November 1968 on an evening when he, as part of Fighter Command, had been put on standby to help with a high security airlift. I've often thought how difficult it must have been for both my parents to be separated at such a time. My father was subject to a complete communications blackout for 24 hours and had no idea how his wife or child were faring. In the end he was given special dispensation to stand down. I do know that I must have come as a bit of a shock though as I had been fondly known as Roger up until the point of my arrival! Trying to agree on a girl's name was not such an easy task for either of them, and it was only just settled on the way to the church for my Christening.

Guernsey Girl

My earliest memories are of helping my father put out prayer and hymn books in our little parish church. I must have been all of about two or three, but I still remember the musty smell of books rarely opened and the thick velvet curtain that tried to keep the draft out of a bitterly cold church. In contrast, the sound I remember is of an aircraft hangar full of men singing hymns at the top of their voices. It was deafening, and quite unlike anything I have ever heard then or since as there were so few treble voices – making my own sound strange and weak in comparison.

It's funny what we remember, isn't it? I also have clear distinct memories of walking to church with my mother and younger sister, Katy, every Sunday once we moved to Crawley. She in a long light blue coat with a fur collar, and Katy and I in our Sunday best. My father was often away as he was now flying for BIA, having finally transitioned into the far less structured civvy-street.

It would be true to say that even at the age of five or six I had a fascination with church. The Sunday School at St Andrew's Church, which was adjacent to our church school, ran a summer mini-mission which I begged to attend – maybe that's why I remember the long walk so much. One of my teachers, whose kind face I can remember even if not her name, said she was committed to praying for me – heaven (quite literally) knows why. For some reason she gave me a little round sticker that boldly stated: 'God Loves You', which I proudly stuck on my half-sized guitar – much, I'm sure, to my parents' horror. Perhaps it had been because of the fervour with which she'd seen me play the Angel Gabriel in the Nativity? (It's interesting to note that Gabriel was definitely seen as a girl's name back then, and it took me quite some time to accept otherwise.)

In 1975, my father secured a job that finally enabled him to fulfil his dream of moving back to Guernsey. This must have been quite a major step for my mother, who was affectionately known as 'the English woman' in the family, but it did introduce

Katy and me to a whole new world of aunts, uncles, cousins and second cousins. Family parties were massive affairs, where the whole island appeared to turn up – because of course everyone was related to each other. We were a clan – and a strong one at that. My dad's older brother, Uncle Lawrie, had been charged by his father to try and keep the family together during the evacuation, and he was committed to ensuring that was the case after it too. Hence the large number of family parties, especially at Christmas.

We initially rented my nan's bungalow, 'Les Affodils' (aptly named because it had been built in a field of daffodils), because it was thought best that she move in to some form of sheltered accommodation. Katy and I were duly enrolled into the Forest Primary School – the same school where my nan had taught, where my father and his siblings had attended before they were evacuated at the start of the war, and at which my mother was soon to become the school secretary.

At first, we went to the main evangelical Anglican church on the island, which was 'in town' at a place called Holy Trinity. However, the logistics of trying to manage Sunday lunches and church started to become quite taxing so in the summer of 1977, following our move out to the country parish of Torteval (even further away from town), my mother decided to take us along to the local Methodist chapel. As I reflect on it now, this decision may also have been affected by the deep-seated church politics which were rife, even in Guernsey. John Wesley had famously come to the island in the late-eighteenth century and had led a massive revival, the legacy of which was that all the 'locals' went to Chapel, while the 'English' went to the Church of England parish churches. Whatever the main reason for the change, we ended up one beautiful sunny morning in Torteval Methodist Chapel. I remember it being quite different, with little gated pews of varying length and a central pulpit, which one had to climb up a staircase to.

Guernsey Girl

The thing I remember most though was that that particular morning there were absolutely no children. My sister and I dutifully sat through the (rather long) service and waited afterwards while mum asked whether there was a Sunday School. Oh yes, they cheerfully explained – but they were all down on the beach at Rocquaine. We rushed home, got our bathers and promptly joined everyone on the sand.

And that's where I met Him.

Well, to be exact, that's where I met the young evangelist who had felt called to spend his summer holiday on the island telling the local youth about Jesus. He was a bronzed, energetic young man with a charismatic personality that meant that we all were enthralled by him. To me he seemed to personify the very Jesus he kept talking about. At the end of the afternoon of games and quizzes I sat on the large beach mat, along with everyone else, listening attentively as he explained that Jesus had come to die for me on a cross, and that I needed to 'welcome Him into my heart'. It all seemed so eminently sensible, thinking about it. Here was the God I had been going to church to worship all these years, and yet had not actually yet got to know personally.

So, when he 'prayed the prayer' and asked us to join in if we too wanted to 'give our lives to the Lord', I closed my eyes and echoed the lines in my head. He then asked those of us who had chosen to do this to stay behind so that he could give us something. A little embarrassed – as most of my friends were now running back down the beach – I stayed and waited while he rummaged in his bag to find a little booklet that explained in more detail what I had just done. I suppose I could have run off, but I knew that God knew that I had prayed the prayer, and there was no hiding from that. He would know – He could see – He was watching. That's what counted.

Later that evening in bed, I took out the little pamphlet and read it from cover to cover. It was quite dated, duplicated on an old mimeograph with a few stencil cartoons of a character that

25

I took to be Jesus. I devoured it quickly as I was an avid reader. Indeed, my fascination for books had nearly cost me my eyesight as I had developed a habit of trying to read by moonlight – until I got caught with my head behind the curtain by my mother one night. I loved adventure books and had read every single Enid Blyton I could get my hands on. So much so that the Head Teacher of my primary school had taken me aside one day to tell me that he thought it would be good for me to give Enid a rest. I remember being quite upset by this – surely it was a good thing I was reading so much? Others in my class just read comics and magazines – at least I read books. In hindsight I can see he thought I was stagnating and wanted me to stretch my mind a little more, which, to be fair, I was already doing having read my way through much of the rather limited school library. However, rather like needing a fix of one's favourite TV serial drama, I needed my Famous Five books just to escape and relax. They created a world where I felt I could belong – in hindsight probably because I related so much to 'George' (aka Georgina). It also taught me, even at the tender age of 9, that adults may have the best intentions but don't always get things right.

Anyway, now I had 'prayed the prayer' I was evidently 'a *proper* Christian'.

I threw myself into Sunday School at chapel, which was made up of about twenty or so children. As I look back now I realise how lucky I was. We were put in classes by age, which meant that I, my best friend Simon and a mutual school friend Paul made up our tiny little class of three. We had our very own teacher, Wendy, who we adored – although to be fair the boys gave her quite a hard time. She patiently unpacked a range of Bible stories and prepared us for our Sunday School tests – which I did rather well in, gaining 100 per cent one year much to our Superintendent's pride.

Guernsey Girl

Music was a big thing for us Methodists – indeed, the thing I remember most is that we sang. We sang everywhere – and anywhere. Our Sunday School choir was legendary, making its mark each year in the Eisteddfod (the island's annual arts festival) under the careful direction of Molly Thompson, a close family friend. On Liberation Day, a public holiday to celebrate the day Guernsey was freed from German Occupation, the whole of chapel would pile into lorries and literally sing ourselves around the island. Because so many of us had been part of the 'Western Music Makers', a children's choir whose sole purpose it seemed was to keep the songs from the 1940s and 1950s alive, we children seemed to know more of the words of the old wartime songs than those who had actually lived through such a dark chapter in history. I have vivid memories of sitting on a rickety old bench at the open end of a tomato truck, sheltered by a loose tarpaulin, while we – the young and old of Torteval – showed the rest of the island 'how it was done'. Health and Safety would now have a field day, but with an island speed limit of 35mph there were rarely any accidents.

It was around this time that Simon, aforementioned best friend, started to learn the violin – which naturally meant that I wanted to do so too. This was just as well as my father had started on a project that was going to become a major hobby in his life – violin making. Although he'd originally set out to make a full-size violin, luckily for me – given a few unfortunate major mishaps along the way – a half-size emerged. This started a love-hate relationship for me with an instrument that I was destined to become quite proficient in. For those who understand the musical grade system, it will make more sense if I explain I achieved my Grade 8 (the top grade) when I was 15, and then spent the next few years 'really learning the violin' as my violin teacher used to put it.

Music became a very significant part of my life, and one in which I found my main social set – be it in island orchestras, Gang Shows, pantomime orchestras, church music groups or on stage at the yearly Eisteddfod. Sadly, the latter was the source of untold levels of stress for me, as I tried valiantly to conquer my nerves while performing solos on stage. Much to my embarrassment this would show very clearly in my right bow arm, which would tremble so badly it seemed I was trying to do some new-fangled oriental sound effect. Miraculously though, the only time I could ever (and still can ever) play on my own in public is when I am lost in worship at church. I have played in front of thousands without a tremor, miked up as a soloist for a variety of worship bands, including at *The Call* in Reading in 2000. But I jump ahead – those days were brought to a crashing end when I came out, and we have a few more years to travel before I get to that part of my story.

In due course I got confirmed at chapel, along with Simon and Paul, marking the end of our time in Sunday School together. The boys were glad to be released from their Sunday commitment, but I wanted more. The natural next step was to join the Sunday night youth group, which I was arguably too young for. However, as with so many other areas of my life, I seemed to be accepted as being older than I actually was and so was allowed to attend. Some nights we met for prayer and bible study, other nights we joined the 'Power, Praise and Healing' meetings in other chapels around the island. These were intense in their worship and devout in their prayer. Visiting preachers were flown onto the island, and together we prayed for 'God's glory to be seen by all'. These were heady days, especially for a young, impressionable, devout teenager like myself.

It was around this time that a dynamic newly ordained Methodist minister called Phil moved to the island with his wife Julie and started a Saturday night youth group called the 'God-Squad'. Many within our small country parish wanted to meet other young Christians, so we arranged lifts and were welcomed in. For my part, Peter, a music master at Elizabeth College (the public boys' school) was also helping to run it, which for me gave it credibility and respectability.

From the very first week we were taught about the gifts of the Holy Spirit, and I longed like others to receive them. One Saturday night I plucked up the courage to ask Phil and Peter to pray for me to be 'baptised in the Holy Spirit', and was therefore taken off to a small quiet room. I am aware how strange this will seem to those of you who have not been party to this type of thing before. It's as though there's a *'Matrix* red pill' moment where those of us who join charismatic churches do so knowing that we will never really speak of it in the 'real world' – not unless we want to be thought of as complete lunatics. Yet I myself was convinced that this was what St Paul had talked about in Corinthians, and what had been prophesied in the book of Joel. It was just a 'normal' part of Christian life for me and for those around me. Many of my older friends were now fluently speaking and singing in tongues, so why not I? They seemed to have pictures and prophetic words for each other, and I wanted to be able to bless those I was praying for with this too.

Phil and Peter explained they were going to ask the Holy Spirit to come, and that all we needed to do was to wait expectantly. They said I might find a strange language coming up from within me, and that I should just 'speak it out'. It must be said that I was slightly nervous. What if nothing happened? What if we prayed and I just sat there? How would I know if what was happening was God or me? I dutifully put my hands out, as though waiting for a gift, and closed my eyes. We prayed. They started speaking in tongues, and I desperately sought around inside my head for any new or strange words that might appear. Nothing. I started to feel embarrassed – all this prayer, just for me. What if it 'failed'? But then, it happened. Out of nowhere words started forming in my head and coming out of mouth – strange foreign words that I had never heard before. They seemed to come from the very core of me, in long almost musical phrases that I found myself repeating over and over again. Words that sounded ancient and yet so familiar.

To this day I have absolutely no idea what these words mean, but I still use them when I'm praying. I find myself repeating them without even thinking, my heart adding differing tonal emphasis depending on who or what I am praying for. Sometimes they bubble up in joy, at other times in deep sorrow, sometimes as a command and yet other times a long heart-felt plea. They have become an almost reflex reaction – particularly in times of distress or nervousness when I automatically find myself speaking them out loud. I remember scaring the living daylights out of my first partner by almost shouting them at a bull that had started to snort and stamp at us as we tried to cross a field on one of our Sunday afternoon walks. I would mutter them under my breath when travelling in dangerous hotspots while abroad, or at the start of a particularly difficult Archbishops' Council meeting. I have no doubt they are a gift – although I am still perplexed as to why some can speak in them and others, no matter how hard they pray, can't.

The one thing left now was for me to get 'baptised' – or should I say, for me to make a public declaration of my faith through the act of giving my testimony and then being fully immersed in water. Like others in our youth group I had been christened (i.e. been baptised as a baby), but none of us saw that as being the same. So, one Sunday night I found myself in a little Baptist church, standing shivering in an old t-shirt and pyjama bottoms. I remember thinking I was lucky it was winter and so the option of doing it in the sea wasn't even talked about. As was the custom in this church, the elders had prayed for each of us before the service (and before even meeting us) and had agreed on a 'baptismal verse' for each of us. Mine was a verse I have 'stood on' (to coin a typical evangelical phrase) throughout my whole Christian life, and the verse that so many people from across the world have 'spoken over me' whenever I have asked them for prayer. I have absolutely no doubt it was the right verse for me, and have held on to it through the most difficult days of my life:

> 'Be strong and courageous. Do not be afraid; do not be discouraged, for the Lord your God will be with you wherever you go.' (Joshua 1:9)

So, I am hoping that by now you are getting the picture of a childhood and adolescence that was steeped in faith and a strong sense of community. My faith was (and still is) undoubtedly the most important thing in my life. I can honestly say I cannot remember a time when I wasn't aware of the presence of Jesus. How amazingly fortunate is that?! Of course, that doesn't mean that I didn't have my doubts, my confusions, and my belly-full of unanswered prayers. But God was and is very real to me. My faith was intense, devout and fervent – like the other young people I was surrounded by, even if they were a fair bit older. I attended as many church meetings as I could organise lifts for – Sunday evening celebrations, weekday prayer meetings, Bible studies, home groups not to mention the annual trip to the Downs Bible Week, where I played in the orchestra.

However, my faith journey was not without its problems. Various people on the island began to get quite concerned about Phil and his colleague, Alan, another local Methodist minister. They had been leading alternative monthly Sunday evening meetings, and together appeared to be spearheading a mini charismatic revival. For the Methodist Circuit this was too much – it was all 'too' charismatic and so they were both asked to leave.[1] Intense discussions ensued, and a decision was made to start The Guernsey Christian Fellowship. This was crunch time. Would people stay in their local Methodist chapels where they had worshipped for years, alongside their friends and neighbours, or would they leave and be part of the 'new thing God was doing'?

Tensions mounted and one morning the *Guernsey Evening Press*, the local paper read by the majority of islanders, chose to run a front-page with a headline stating that the Moonies were attempting to brainwash the island's youth! As a result, I and others under 16 were banned from attending any more meetings. In a fit of pique, I swung to the 'other end of the candle' and joined the Town Church Choir, the island's nearest thing to a Cathedral Choir. As it happened, the church organist was Peter – the teacher who had prayed for me to be baptised in the Holy Spirit – and so I still felt somewhat at home, even if things couldn't have been more different liturgically.

I know my mother was particularly concerned about whether I had been caught up in some form of 'cult', and so sat me down at the kitchen table one evening and asked me to read a section of the New Testament out loud. I was highly embarrassed and quite frankly, angry. Even though I knew she was doing this out of a great concern for my wellbeing, I found it laughable that she thought that if I had a demon I would not be able to read scripture out aloud.

Over time my parents relented, and I was allowed to attend week-day prayer meetings, and then eventually Sunday services where I was part of the worship group with Eileen, a cellist, and one of our next-door neighbours in Torteval. There were, however, three defining events that were soon to happen, which would affect and scar my relationship with 'the Church' for many years to come.

---

[1] 'Charismatic' is a term used to describe churches which placed a greater emphasis on gifts and manifestations of the Holy Spirit. A worldwide growth of such congregations in the latter half of the twentieth century was viewed with some concern among some church communities.

Guernsey Girl

The first involved the wedding of two of my closest friends who were involved with our church. I remember the absolute thrill of being asked to be my friend's bridesmaid, and then the huge sadness of learning that her parents had decided to boycott her wedding. They didn't approve of this new style of church, with our modern worship songs and a more informal approach to service structure. It was not something that their church recognised and so they would not attend.

It was tragic and heart-breaking. Our church community gathered round and put on one of the finest wedding banquets I've ever been to, but it was obviously not the same. The day was spent wondering whether her father would acquiesce, a tension that I know weighed heavily on my dear friend's mind during what should have been the happiest day of her life. Fortunately, her mother did come, and her uncle gave her away. It was a harsh lesson in life for me though: when it comes to belief, people can be extremely dogmatic, even if it affects their nearest and dearest.

It taught me that while so many people believe they need to 'stand firm against the devil', they do so forgetting that that the devil is rarely found in others, but rather in our own cold and judgemental attitudes. You see, I don't believe that God ever needs defending – He is more than capable of defending Himself. However, He does need us to be His agents of His love and grace.

The second event was just as heart-breaking, if not more so, but for a completely different reason. Mark Brehaut was one of the kindest, funniest and bravest young men in our Torteval chapel Sunday School. His father lived in a huge old Guernsey farmhouse 'down the hill' on the way to the beach. Simon and I used to spend hours playing hide and seek there and, although Mark was a good four or five years older than us (a massive age gap when you're young), he was still up for spending time with us. He was the first to get a car – an old red Ford Capri with woolly dice dangling from the mirror and a shaggy rug that covered the back seat. He'd take us for rides, and sometimes even let us change the gears. Then one day he got toothache, really bad toothache. Like most young men he left it – for far too long. By the time the GP saw him he was in agony – but that was the least of his problems. His blood tests showed something far more sinister – he had cancer, leukaemia to be precise. It seemed impossible. Cancer? At his age? He was so young and fit. He was from Guernsey, where nothing much ever happened to anyone. This was the early 1980s and cancer was just creeping into everyone's consciousness. It was a total bombshell.

Mark went over to Southampton for treatment, and we committed ourselves to pray. It felt like we had been sent on a mission – a critical one, on which a close friend's very life depended. He would come back to the island every so often, his thick dark hair now gone and replaced by a few long wispy strands, making him look like an old oriental opium dealer. He asked if he could come to The Guernsey Christian Fellowship with us on Sunday mornings, and so the Hottons – who kindly used to drive us there each week – squeezed him into the car with us.

And then a miracle happened. He got better! Miraculously better! Gosh, even now I remember the leap in my heart when we heard the wonderful news. His white blood cell count improved significantly – no one could quite believe it, least of all Mark. There was hope. But then it all came to a crashing halt. His remission, for that is what it had been, suddenly came to an end.

Mark died very shortly after that.

We weren't allowed to go to the funeral. We were thought to be too young. So, we just stood outside the chapel in protest, motivated by our desire to pay our own last respects to our friend.

Please don't ever try to shield young people from death. It's a part of life. The hardest thing was losing him, the second hardest thing was not being able to say goodbye. I was angry, confused – both with God and those who had made such a decision on our behalf. Where had God been? What was He playing at? Why had He given us such hope for it all to be dashed so quickly?

And so, an even more important lesson in life was learnt – life just isn't fair. It can hurt!

———••———

The final event was really two distinct events, but they will be forever linked in my mind. The scars of these were to go deeper than anything that had happened before, and lead me to stop going to church for most of my time in Cambridge. I just didn't know who to trust any more.

It must have been during my sixth form years that the first event happened. One Sunday at the start of the service, we were all told that there was to be an emergency church meeting at the end, which we would all be required to attend.

I wonder now who else knew what was about to happen? The elders, obviously – but others? I certainly knew nothing. The only thing that surprised me was that our worship leader wasn't playing his guitar in the worship band and was instead sat next to his girlfriend. I had known them both for some time as they too had been part of the God-Squad. Writing this now, my heart goes out to them – how on earth did they get through that service? I so wish I could turn the clock back and stop it there and then. We should have done, all of us should have done.

At the end, after the final prayer, all those who weren't official 'church members' were asked to leave. The doors were closed, and the elders stood up. They explained that they had some very upsetting news to share – that my friend had become pregnant by her boyfriend. They were publicly chastised and told they would be removed from all church leadership positions. My memory tells me that we were then told they were to be put outside the Church for a period. I can't believe we could have been so callous – surely, we would have supported them through this difficult time? Guernsey is a small place, and rumours spread fast. Were we really that harsh? I fear we were. I know I felt powerless to stop anything. We felt their shame, and the warning was crystal clear – this is what happens if you cross the line. Be warned!

A couple of years later, just months before I was to leave the island for Cambridge, the second thing happened. Or rather, I learnt about it. One of our elders was having an affair. He had been for some time. I was apoplectic. The hypocrisy! The humiliation! Hadn't we left our parish chapels, been called names in the press, been through heartache in our families to join a church – one that had taken such a hard stance against my dear pregnant friend – led by a philanderer!

Yes, I realise I'm still angry.

No, I didn't want anything more to do with the charismatic church – not for a very long time anyway.

CHAPTER TWO

The School of Life

Summer 1987

One small fact that might have been a bit of a give-away to my burgeoning sexuality is that my best mates were always guys – they still are.

I honestly can't remember a time while growing up when I didn't have a best male buddy – from my early playschool days in Crawley with Roland, to my primary school days in Guernsey with Simon, to my secondary school days with Steven and then to university with David. It perhaps won't surprise you to learn therefore that I was an ardent tom-boy, who absolutely hated playing with dolls (as I just couldn't see the point) unless it was, of course, my beloved Action Girl.

My earliest memories at Forest Primary School were of playing football with the boys during breaktime. This was unheard of before my arrival, but the truth was that I was quite good, and fearless in the face of 'Bim' – a very talented young footballer who no one liked to tackle. As we got older and the gender stereotyping became clearer – boys did woodwork and played cricket while girls did needlework and played netball – I became increasingly frustrated. The differences between the sexes was most apparent in our after-school activities, where the Cubs and Scouts seemed to me to have far more adventures than the Brownies and Guides. It is true that I longed to be a boy – for no other reason than they always seemed to have all the fun: sailing, rock climbing, fishing, canoeing. I'd have never sought to change my sex though – my frustrations were far more with the social norms than with inner conflicts.

Simon, my partner in crime in so many adventures, helped make up for all this. Together we made dens, real dens – first in an old hay loft, then converting an old pig sty and installing our handmade 3-D periscope. We went snorkelling for ormers, clay pigeon hunting on the cliffs (where we'd sell the recovered clays back to their owners) and fishing off Fort Grey. We would get purposefully lost in the maize fields, and then try to navigate our way out using the sun. We had countless sleepovers, which always involved midnight feasts (although neither of us ever felt that hungry at two o'clock in the morning), and spent goodness knows how many hours playing Escape from Colditz.

According to our parents, we never once argued. Simon was just that bit older than me and I was a very willing Number 2 in everything we did. I learnt to fast bowl so that he could practise his cricket, and stood nervously in goal while he fired ball after ball at me, kicking with increasing strength as he got older. Eventually, however, peer pressure took over and once at secondary school we found ourselves going our own ways. Having a girl as (just) a friend really was not that cool.

Sadly, Simon died of a brain haemorrhage a couple of years ago. We had tried to stay in touch as best we could, and I was glad to see him whenever I returned to the island to see my parents as I knew he was incredibly lonely. On arriving at the crematorium for the funeral I remember passing lines of cars double parked as hundreds of his old friends turned up to pay their last respects. I had crumbled, wondering where on earth they had all been when he needed them?

It was a salutary lesson in loneliness – a beast that has stalked me for a very significant part of my life, and still does. You can have lots of folk who know you, who will miss you when you're gone, but very few really close friends who are actually there for you when times get tough.

True friends are hard to find. Hold them close and treasure them when you do.

The School of Life

Reflecting back on my childhood, I think one of the problems that I and other 'bright' kids had was that we were often 'put up a year' at the start of our time at primary school, which meant that we then had to repeat a year in the top class. This meant that we lost all our natural friends, who went on to bigger and better things at secondary school. In my case it also meant I ended up spending a year in my sister's class, as she was in the year below me (having also been put up a year). This felt quite demeaning. What is more, Simon had spent his last year of primary school at Beechwood, the boy's prep school to Elizabeth College, so he was no longer at the Forest anyway.

I got a scholarship, as I was expected to, to the Ladies' College. We still had the 11-Plus in those days, which awarded scholarships to either Elizabeth College, Ladies' College or Blanchelande, the girl's Catholic private school, where most of my music friends were boarders. If you 'passed' you went to the Boys' or Girls' Grammar Schools, and if you 'failed' you went to your nearest comprehensive. Oh, the seeming innocence of it all back then. One day we would just turn up to school and the desks would all be separated into isolated islands in the classroom. We would sit down, do the test and then go out to play. I must admit to being quite surprised when I got to Ladies' College and learnt that the other girls had been coached – either by their schools or in private lessons. They had known exactly when the exam was going to be and what to expect with it all. They seemed to think me very strange for not having had the same.

I started at the Ladies' College with two other girls from the Forest – Tracey and Louise, the first of whom had had a scholarship like me, the latter was fee-paying. We really felt like 'country bumpkins' next to all the posh private school girls, and I remember wondering if I was really going to be cut out for it all. The first set of exams proved otherwise though, and I soon realised that I had a rather different problem to deal with. Having come top in virtually every exam except English Language (where I had come 24th out of 28, an anomaly that was not lost on my Form Teacher, who thought my English teacher's marking very strange), I realised I was going to have to navigate a careful path between being very bright and still being liked by my classmates.

The truth is, however, I had very little in common with them. I was musical – they were not. In fact, I was the only girl in the class to play in the school orchestra or sing in either of the two choirs. I was a Christian, actively involved with the Christian Union, most were not. I was in the Drama Society, for which I ran the school's breaktime Tuck Shop – the others were not. They were all sports mad – and I most definitely was not. In fact, I hated 'girly sports', especially hockey where because of my size I was frequently put in goal, the ideal target for their 'innocent' practice.

I realise now how incredibly alienated and isolated I felt, although I just accepted this as 'normal'. It formed various character traits within me, which are still there if you look closely – from overly apologising to attempting to downplay my abilities. I had little self-esteem, let alone sense of self-worth, which was not helped by a world in which it was rare to praise or encourage a gifted child in case they got too 'big-headed'. The burden of being bright (when it really wasn't fashionable to be so) felt crushing – and only succeeded in undermining my self-confidence further. I tried to laugh my way out of the bullying that inevitably occurred and learnt instead to play the fool. During my private prayer times I would endeavour to 'give it all back to God' and worked hard at trying to 'love them anyway'. But their teasing and jibes hurt, deeply, and there seemed little or nothing I could do about it. It was obviously all my fault, and yet I couldn't see why.

Of course, there was one even greater difference which

The School of Life

I was completely unaware of and would remain in blissful ignorance of for some time – I just wasn't interested in boys, well not in the way that the other girls were. I recognise now that I was completely shut down sexually. I had no idea what physical attraction was, although I constantly kept being told at church that this was something I should be very wary of and needed to learn to control. At heart I saw myself as a true romantic and longed for the day I would 'fall in love' with that warm giddy feeling that would knock me off my feet. I wanted that 'Hollywood moment' where my eyes would meet someone, preferably whilst watching a sunset, and where the music would build to a crescendo while the lights faded.

The only time I felt a flicker of anything vaguely resembling this was, rather ironically, the day I auditioned for the school orchestra, just after joining Ladies' College. I was extremely nervous about this – I had never played in an orchestra before, and I thought that as one of the youngest violinists in the school I wouldn't be good enough. The teacher in charge of the orchestra was Mrs Colley, whose elder daughter Lydia had just been awarded a music scholarship at Oxford. I remember the day this was announced in assembly – although few of us understood what she had achieved, we knew it had to be something very significant as the whole school was given a special day off to celebrate. Lydia was my hero, or should I say heroine. Unbeknown to me, Mrs Colley had invited her in to listen to my audition and so after I finished playing my specially prepared piece, the 'Londonderry Air', Lydia came up to congratulate me. I remember going white and nearly swooning. Could this really be happening? This beautiful, clever, talented woman was actually talking to me. At the time I just put it down to what I had read to be a 'girl crush', but with hindsight I now realise that she was exactly 'my type'! For the record, the audition must have gone well as I found myself on the front desk in my very first rehearsal, desperately trying to hear the sound of my violin over the swirl of music around me. It was a very steep learning curve.

Just Love

I worked hard and endeavoured to lead a full life. Given I had so little to connect me to my classmates, I wrapped myself up in my faith. I would either join the older girls from my church for a lunchtime prayer meeting when I could, or busy myself with some other lunch time activity.

The main change to the routine came when I started playing in pit orchestras for GADOC, the Guernsey's Amateur Dramatic and Operatic Company. This opened up a whole new group of friends – as usual far older than me, but friends with whom I could be accepted for who I was. I relished being part of 'a company'. I loved the thrill of the curtain going up, the sense of camaraderie on stage, the fact I was part of something – and the laughter. Boy we laughed – on stage, off stage, in rehearsals and most memorably of all in the pit itself when we tried to tease the pantomime dame by mixing up all 'her' prompt sheets. These were surreptitiously pinned to the inside of our surrounding curtain so that they could be read by whoever was on stage, but not by the audience. In return, those on stage would get their own back – by throwing things at us or by ensuring that the maximum amount of dry ice was pumped on stage during the interval so that when the curtains went up it would pour down into the pit, blinding us and making us cough.

Inevitably, time marched on and I started to think about my future. At this stage I had little clarity about what I wanted to do or be, but I did know which subject I enjoyed the most. I therefore set my heart on going to Cambridge to study mathematics. Interestingly, although I was good at physics – and did rather well in the British Physics Olympiad – I was never encouraged to think of studying either physics or engineering. Girls just didn't do that sort of thing in my day.

However, my Cambridge dream was going to require a bit of a miracle as my maths teacher did not have the best record of getting girls through their A Level, let alone their Further Maths or S Level papers. This small problem was exacerbated by the fact that my mother was now a maths teacher at my school, teaching girls up to O Level, and it was her boss who was teaching me. At a school reunion recently, my old class mates gratefully recounted how I used to repeat entire maths lessons for them in order that they might get their heads around what they should have been taught in the previous periods. I was not impressed but complaining was not an option.

Fortunately for me, help was to come from a completely different route.

I remember meeting Steven at a disco at La Trelade, a hotel that used to put on events for the over-sixteens. This really wasn't my scene, but as my other friends from Youth Orchestra were all going, I thought it best to try and make an effort so as to fit in. Steven was my age, and in many ways my exact equivalent – even if we weren't to understand how much so for some time. The only obvious difference was that he was at Elizabeth College and a Catholic, rather than a mad charismatic like myself. We talked – non-stop, about anything and everything. We took each other's phone number, and talked more – for hours, at length, which is how I anticipated the other girls in my class interacted with their male friends. The only thing was that we weren't remotely romantically interested in each other, although everyone of course assumed that we were. No – we were 'just friends'. He seemed like an older version of my dear friend Simon, with me once again happily playing second fiddle.

Steven's dream was to read mathematics at Oxford – a dream he would soon realise before becoming one of the finest mathematicians of his year there. He would then go on to study at Berkeley, California, before founding several maths-orientated start-ups in Silicon Valley. A truly brilliant mathematician – and the prodigy of his school maths teacher, Robert.

The three of us, Robert, Steven and I, formed a very unlikely trio – well, perhaps not that unlikely, but certainly unusual.

Robert spoilt us rotten, introducing us to a 'Brideshead Revisited' way of life that we both craved. We consumed countless bottles of fizz and ate (at his expense) at some of the best restaurants on the island – of which there were many. He also helped us prepare for our Oxbridge entrance papers. For me, this was to involve a new system of S Level papers that no one had been through before, so I felt totally in the dark. I realised Robert's focus was really on Steven, but I learnt from their exchanges and so found a version of the tuition I so desperately needed.

Now, at this point I think I should admit that I had fallen hopelessly and madly in love with Robert. He was everything I thought I wanted in a man – clever, sophisticated, with exquisite taste in clothes, art and music. He seemed so refined, and just the debonair type of guy I was after, or at least I thought I was. Yes, he was quite effeminate – but that's what I found so attractive. The truth was that this was the first of many unrequited relationships for me with gay men ... the only problem was that I could never see that they were gay, I just didn't believe people could be.

I say that, but I suppose I did realise that some men could be – after all, this was the 1980s and so we had the likes of John Inman and Kenneth Williams to laugh at on our television screens (sadly, gay men were almost always the target of the jokes back then). But 'ordinary' people weren't gay – people I knew weren't gay, and most definitely women weren't gay. I mean this. As surprising as it may sound, I truly didn't know that women could be gay. Yes, I had heard rumours of some

44

women who acted like men – we had such a girl in our sixth form when I started school – but that was really rare.

Women were meant to conform, even if men didn't, and settle down and have kids.

Steven kept trying to tell me the truth about Robert, but I didn't want to know – I didn't want my 'bubble to burst'. It's very ironic to think now that out of the six boys I knew from Elizabeth College – all of whom I formed a good friendship group with – four turned out to be gay. Was there something in the water? I think perhaps our parents thought so ....

I didn't realise Steven was gay until I went to visit him at Oxford when I was at Cambridge. I knew he had always questioned whether he might be, but deep down I thought this was just a phase he – like others – was going through, and that he would 'get over it' in time.

I'll be honest – I couldn't wait to leave the island.

I had been suffering from something akin to an intense bout of cabin fever for years. I was desperate to get away and be free of all that kept me trapped and boxed.

I did well in my A Levels, but not quite well enough. Sadly, I was just one point short of the grades I needed – I had got the three A grades needed at A level, but I had not got a first in either of my S Papers. I remember reading the results, staring at the form thinking 'so near, but yet so far'.

I was bitterly disappointed, but somehow deep down I *knew* that I was meant to be going to Cambridge. I hadn't a clue how this would happen, especially because I knew the chances of them relenting were very slim. St John's College, the Cambridge college I had applied to, was always oversubscribed with applicants and frequently offered more places than they had spaces for.

The only slight glimmer of hope was that I had also tried for a music scholarship because St John's was one of the best known musical colleges – as well as one of the top colleges for maths. Sadly, though I felt the audition had not gone well. I had been made to feel an utter fool in the sight-reading test, which presented me with one of the hardest pieces of music I have ever seen in my life.

The one thing going in my favour, which hadn't really crossed my mind, was the fact that St John's College had only just gone mixed and had a terrible record of encouraging female mathematicians. The powers that be therefore decided to acquiesce and let Mary, an incredibly sporty dyslexic rower, and me in. Sadly, as you can imagine, dyslexia and mathematics aren't the best combination, and so unfortunately Mary didn't make it past the first year. I was therefore left to hold the fort – the sole female amongst fifteen mathematicians in my College year group.

Maths at Cambridge was hard, much harder than I had realised it would be.

It seemed that most of my fellow class mates had all received additional teaching at their secondary schools in preparation for their first year, and were therefore far better equipped than me. What's more there were no books to help. It appeared that a standard degree course in mathematics was covered in virtually the first year, meaning that the second and third years were well beyond most degrees and consequently there were no books readily available.

Yes, we were studying some of the most cutting-edge concepts in mathematics and being taught by some of the greatest minds of our time, but this did not mean that they were good teachers. In fact, the standard of teaching was abysmal. While this seemed normal back then, today it would be viewed as completely unacceptable.

To counter this, the students developed their own way of dealing with substandard teaching. I remember one poor lecturer in pure maths who I think was on the verge of a nervous breakdown. He should never have been let loose in front of a hundred bright – mostly male – students. Chalk stealing, waterbombs, cat calling – you name it, the guys made his life hell. For my part, I just sat at the back and took as many notes as I could, hoping that one day it would all make some sense.

Mathematicians are a very varied bunch. I myself rarely admit to being one because of the image it frequently brings up in people's minds. Now that Asperger's syndrome has become more recognised and understood, I would offer that many of the 'mathmos' in my college were 'on the spectrum'.

I remember my mother coming over to visit me once and discovering this the hard way. She was waiting for me at the exit to the lecture room at the end of one of my lectures. Given I preferred sitting at the back I was always one of the last to leave, and by the time I got to her she was in shock. Why were there so many unwashed, unshaven, unkempt young men? I explained that that was just the way things were – genius came in many forms, but it did often seem to have an eccentric side to it.

My saving grace came in the form of a lovely young man called David. We met on our first day at Cambridge, well his first and my second. I had come over from Guernsey on the overnight boat, so had actually arrived in college a day early. This meant I was completely settled in by the time that the others on my floor arrived – and I could therefore go around offering cups of tea as a bribe to try and make some new friends. David was one of the first to arrive, having driven down from Wakefield with his parents, and they accepted 'a cuppa' willingly. This was to start the closest friendship I had during my time at Cambridge – another purely platonic relationship, but one that would mean so much. The best thing was that we were both studying maths.

We soon became inseparable – walking to lectures, struggling over test papers, drinking in the bar, going to formal hall. A year later David was to go out with my best female friend, Bridgeen, but that was fine – it was like my brother dating a very good friend.

It was thanks to David that I got to hear about a brilliant mathematics professor who was giving a series of lectures in our first year on a book he had written to try and prove there wasn't a God. David explained that it might be a little difficult to follow as the lecturer had to speak with a voice box, but we went all the same. I now realise that Professor Hawking was basically reading out *A Brief History of Time*. This soon-to-be world bestseller – the book that everyone would buy, but almost no one would read – was being tried out on us. I lasted one lecture, having got lost after about twenty minutes. I so wish now I'd stayed the course – but I did at least buy, read and finish the book!

But this did not diminish the fact that I found maths unenjoyably difficult. Things were not made any easier by our college supervisors – one of whom had very wandering hands when he got drunk, as I was to find out at our tutor's Christmas drinks party. This was extremely awkward. I naturally made a fuss and complained, which set me on a path of writing about the Welfare System in the College (or rather, the lack of it). If a young woman like myself was groped by a senior fellow, would she really feel able to go and talk to her College Tutor, who was supposedly in charge of her welfare, but was actually one of the perpetrator's close mates? Of course not, as I was to find to my cost. (Ironically as I write this I am in the process of trying to get the Church of England to recognise a very similar problem – that unless one has a completely independent safeguarding system it will fail the victim from the start, and so most won't bother to complain.)

For me, this was made even harder when I found myself elected to the College Council as one of the JCR representatives. Here I found myself having to sit alongside my lecherous supervisor, my tutor and the college chaplain – all of whom knew exactly what had happened and had helped to cover it up. At least the tradition of 'roasting', where the two student reps were placed in full academic dress in front of a roaring fire for the length of the College Council meeting (ostensibly to 'complete the fourth side of the square' that their three tables made, but mostly for the amusement of the fellows) meant that my red face was put down to the heat and not my shame.

The good news, however, was that I was the first woman to get on to the College Council – and I was going to make them face up to a few things whether they wanted to or not: the lack of toilets and bathrooms on staircases (we were still expected to walk across a quad in our dressing gowns), the lack of mirrors, and the poor lighting on The Backs (the area on the far side of the river), which had made it a dangerous place for students returning from the library. I was on a crusade and having made a good working relationship with the Domestic Bursar, we worked together to bring the college into the twentieth century.

I must admit that the thing I was proudest of achieving during my time there was a way to ensure that the Post Room could be kept open during meal times so that students entering into college could collect their post. A bit of a no-brainer you might think, but because the porters wanted to eat they used to lock everything up at the very time students were coming in. All it needed was a creative solution and some good-will on all sides.

It was the start of my activism – I suppose that deep down I've always been a change maker.

On reflection, my university days were relatively uneventful – certainly on the romantic front. I kept hoping to meet someone, but no one seemed to be that interested in me – and on reflection, there wasn't any one who I was that attracted to. I toyed with the idea of dating a couple of guys, and actually went to a dinner with one, but nothing came of it.

I suppose the craziest things that happened were those to do with my future career plans. Specifically, there were three rather unusual events occurred in quick succession in my final year.

At the start of the Michaelmas (or autumn) Term I received a crisp white envelope with a rather surprising letter inside. It was from a company called 'Procter & Gamble' who were inviting me to join them for an all-inclusive week in a 4-star hotel in Windsor to learn about marketing. I thought it was a joke. In fact, I thought it was a rather eccentric hoax by an old Guernsey friend, David, who was at that point taking time out to work for the Industrial Society. I rang him (not that easy to do in those days) using something that is now nearly extinct – a pay phone – and laughingly said I had nearly fallen for it. After a few minutes of confused exchanges, I began to realise that this letter might actually be for real, and that David was really impressed that I had received one.

The truth is that I had, without meaning to, worked up quite a reputation in Cambridge, which is how they must have heard about me. I had run various college societies (including a wine tasting society, set up in memoriam of a fellow who left money in his will to teach students about the finer aspects of wine), overseen a college rent strike, fought to keep the College bar open and told the Oxford and Cambridge Society where to go with their extremely sexist admissions policy.

The latter event stemmed from a rather unfortunate mistake on their part. I had been invited to a drinks evening for JCR officials, where they had (wrongly) assumed that their guests from the large male-dominated colleges would in fact be all male. I turned up, much to their surprise I recall, and on hearing the policy that female members were not allowed in certain parts of the club, told them in no uncertain terms how disgraceful this was. I reminded them that we were living 'in an age when our prime minister is female, our monarch is female and the prime minister of the largest Islamic democracy in the world, is female'. Needless to say, I didn't get a follow-up letter.

I had by now set my heart on joining the Foreign Office so that I could be a 'Voice for the Voiceless'. However, a week's full board in a 4-star hotel was not to be sniffed at and since David had assured me I would definitely enjoy it, I decided to give the marketing 'taster' a go.

We were told repeatedly from the outset that this was not in any way an interview and that no assessment of any participant would be taking place. I naively believed that. It was only when I received a follow-up invitation to meet with some of the Procter & Gamble managers, followed promptly by an immediate job offer, that I realised that of course they had been watching.

Much to their amazement, I declined.

With hindsight this was quite a shrewd move on my part as it meant I was then wined and dined at some of the best restaurants in Cambridge for next two terms, as various members of the company tried to persuade me to reconsider. They were also quite bemused – no one had ever turned them down before, indeed candidates were normally begging them to join.

Procter & Gamble is still seen by many as the top blue-chip marketing company, owning a range of major household brand names like Ariel, Pampers, Flash and Fairy Liquid. Indeed, it was a company that most business students would give their eye-teeth to work for. However, I was clear – there was no way I was going to work for a 'big bad corporate giant', who had just been in the news for having a logo that seemingly incorporated the Great Satan himself![1]

------•◆•------

[1] The Procter & Gamble 'Moon and Stars' logo attracted controversy in the 1980s as a myth started to circulate stating that its true meaning was of a horned ram with 13 stars (reference to Revelation 12:1), and an inverted 666 symbol. Unable to quash the rumours the company had changed its logo in 1985.

I now need to jump back in time just a bit and explain that at the end of my second year I had been approached by a senior fellow at my college and asked if I would mind joining him for tea in his rooms later that week. Slightly nervous but rather curious, I went at the appointed time and learnt that this fellow 'had friends in London' who were keen to meet me as they understood I had sat the Foreign Office entrance exams.

Intrigued, I agreed to go, and so found myself in some hushed rooms off The Mall with a stunning view of Buckingham Palace. Our discussions went well, and so I agreed to a second interview on the return from my summer holidays. I was flattered, but conflicted. At their suggestion, I had gone to see my College Dean of Divinity (another of 'their friends'!) to talk things through in more depth. I concluded, however, that no matter how great the cause I just couldn't live a double life.

You see, if there's one thing that forms the very core of who I am, it's that I find it virtually impossible to lie. I act as one large human lie detector machine – my heart starts to pound; my cheeks go red and a big red rash starts to creep down my neck (which, to be fair, also happens when I'm stressed or nervous). I would reflect on this fact over the years to come as I struggled with my sexuality. Indeed, it's what eventually led me to come out – I just couldn't live a lie.

Ironically, my intelligence friends had come to the same conclusion. They advised me that I would probably find waiting to fill 'dead men's shoes' in the Foreign Office rather boring, and that on reflection I would be far better off going to work for Procter & Gamble. The alternative, they explained, was that if I accepted their offer I would be sent to a Middle Eastern country to learn Arabic. That didn't sound too much fun to me, especially as a woman.

I can see now, however, I was just their type – someone who could network and fit in with any group, but who was also a bit of a loner, and who could exist quite happily on their own.

The School of Life

My over-riding desire was to do whatever Mr God (a term I adopted, after reading the book *Mister God, This is Anna*) wanted me to do. At the time I had a strong belief that there was either a 'right path' or a 'wrong path', and I was therefore at pains to try and discern which was which.

Given the events in Guernsey, I had assiduously avoided the Christian Union while at Cambridge and, to a large part, the Round Church – which was under the watchful eyes of Mark Rushton and Giles Walter. However, my faith remained strong and I surrounded myself with mostly Christian friends. Together we attended Chapel Breakfast on a Sunday morning – a free cooked breakfast for those who made the 8am Eucharist, which was a tall order after a late Saturday night.

It was during one of these early morning Chapel services that I had what seemed like a perfectly normal idea of writing to the one person I thought it would be good to work for, given his strategic future role in the country. I therefore put pen to paper and wrote what has to be one of the most 'out there' letters. Much to my amazement I received a reply, which I still have framed on my office wall. I wish I could meet Mrs John Denman, the Personnel Officer, as her turn of phrase was exquisite. Typed neatly on St James' Palace headed note paper she started it by saying:

> '*I have been asked by The Prince of Wales to write and thank you for your letter. We were very interested to read your letter. Sadly, His Royal Highness' Office is rather small, and there are no areas in which we feel we would be able to make use of your various talents....*'

Priceless.

Time was drawing in and I needed to decide what to do. I really struggled with the concept of working for Procter & Gamble, and so – like Gideon – I laid out a fleece and asked for a sign.[2]

The signs (plural) came thick and fast.

Firstly, my old friend Steven (now also in his final year at Jesus College, Oxford) introduced me to his college chapel friend, Jo. Her parents just happened to live in Newcastle-upon-Tyne, where Procter & Gamble was based. They were all devout Methodists, and felt they were meant to offer me free board and lodgings should I ever need it while 'finding my feet' up there. Then, later that summer while helping out at Rushmore (a Christian girl's camp that was the partner to the infamous Iwerne Trust boys' camp), I found myself sharing a room with a woman called Sue who worked for – you guessed it – Procter & Gamble. Evidently, according to her, I was down to take over from her as Brand Assistant on Fairy Liquid if and when I accepted the post.

This was just one too many coincidences, even for me, so I accepted the job offer and made plans to move 'up north' – the furthest I'd been yet from Guernsey.

I can't help smiling now as I look back at this time – that God definitely has one very large sense of humour. Knowing hardly anyone in Newcastle, I decided to get involved with the large evangelical church that was situated virtually next door to where I was staying in the parish of Jesmond – none other than Jesmond Parish Church. As it turned out Sue and a couple of other new friends from work also went there, although to be fair none of us women got on that well with the vicar – one Revd David Holloway and his curate, the Revd Jonathan Pryke!

---

[2] The Old Testament tells the story of Gideon (Judges 6: 36-40) who, unsure whether God is really calling him to do something, puts out a fleece of wool on dry ground and prays that God will give him a sign by making the fleece wet in the morning and the ground dry. This happens. Unsure, he repeats the test again, and again God answers his prayer.

The School of Life

Procter & Gamble had a yearly intake of new Brand Assistants, all of whom started in early September – almost like a new academic school year. From memory there were about twelve of us, from a diverse set of backgrounds but with a disproportionate number of Oxbridge graduates.

Out of this intake I made one really good friend, a great guy called Jonathan, who like David and Steven before him was to be my 'best buddy'. Although we were teased mercilessly by the P&G crowd, given they wrongly assumed we were secretly dating, we stood by each other.

This was a highly competitive market place, where none of us were under any disillusionment that this was a form of 'Hunger Games' as the company operated an aggressive 'up or out' policy. This meant that if you weren't on track for promotion then you needed to start looking elsewhere.

My first day of work is marked in history as the start of the 'Soap Sud Wars', where Unilever decided to launch a full-on attack on their major rival's cash cow – Fairy Liquid. With the trade a hundred per cent behind them (given the low margins we offered on this 'known value item' that 70 per cent of households used), their aim was to build on the successful Persil detergent brand and launch Persil Dishwashing Liquid in a trendy new bottle with the help of comedian and actor Robbie Coltrane.

The gloves were off!

Up till that point, Fairy Liquid had only ever had to advertise on TV to keep its market share. Our adverts were legendary – from 'Mummy, mummy why are your hands so soft?' to Nanette Newman showing how many more school dinner tables of plates we could wash up compared to the nearest competitor. But this 'war' required a far stronger defence strategy – one that would rigorously protect our market share, even if it would cost us $50m to do so.

It was my boss who came up with the ultimate solution – load consumers with so much washing up liquid that they couldn't possibly want to buy any more during the Persil launch phase. This was deemed even more necessary when we learnt that Unilever were about to have a Try Me Free Offer. This was therefore how the 'BOGOF' – as it is now fondly known – was born: as far as I am aware we were the first major Buy One Get One Free on a large household brand.

As the brand assistant in charge of 'making things happen', I was pulled into a summit meeting with our General Manager, Mike Clasper, and asked what it would take to ensure that we beat the competition onto the shelf with our offer. Given their launch was only eight weeks away and most projects took four months, it seemed a near impossible task. The scenario was made even more surreal by the fact that Mike had completely lost his voice and was writing all his questions onto a large flip chart in the London boardroom of our advertising agency, Grey. I explained that I needed something to show I had his authority to make this the most important project in the company, and that it could take precedence over everything else. He smiled, reached for his notepad, and simply wrote 'I agree everything, Mike'. Holding this precious 'golden ticket' I jumped on the train back home and set to work, knowing it was not just the future of Fairy Liquid that was at stake.

Two months later, we matched them on-shelf and in the majority of the nation's letterboxes. The latter involved a coupon drop that claimed we were '8 days/8 ways better' than the new trendy shaped bottle, clearly identifiable as Persil. This was a brave move, particularly for a risk-adverse P&G. Unilever took us to court, but we won. I received praise from our global head, Mr Ed Artz himself, and found myself the first to be promoted in my year, achieving the coveted 5-star rating.

It was quite a start to my career – but all was not to stay rosy for long.

Sadly, an event was about to occur that would change my life and leave its scars for years to come.

The School of Life

As with university, I set my goals high and worked hard to achieve them, frequently having to deal with the inner clamours of crippling self-doubt that led me to think I would constantly fail. It was the same inner voice that would tell me that I was unattractive and ugly, and that no one would ever be interested in me – a theme that had stalked me throughout my life to date.

The incident involved someone who I had met while I was at Cambridge and who was now a curate in the Church of England. We had become good friends, indeed 'very good friends' – although to be fair I wasn't at all clear as to the exact nature of our 'friendship'. Were we going out? He didn't seem to think so, and there was certainly never any talk about what either of us were feeling or indeed of love. However, for me, the whole scenario was made desperately more complicated by the fact that he was the first man who had ever shown any interest in me sexually.

I found this both flattering and intriguing, indeed somewhat also of a relief especially given I had begun to think that there had to be something wrong with me. 'Why weren't guys asking me out?' I kept wondering. It didn't cross my mind that it might be because I wasn't showing any interest in any of them – well, not the kind of interest that they were used to from a woman.

By the time he came to visit me in Newcastle we had known each other for about two years, during which time we had argued constantly about whether sex was just for marriage or not. For my part, I was crystal clear on this point – it was the biblical expectation that a woman would give herself solely to her husband, and not until they were married. Indeed, the gift of my virginity was I believed the most precious wedding gift I could ever think of giving my husband.

Like so many other young evangelical Christians though, I was keen to understand just 'how far you could go' without overstepping this important red line. I felt totally ill-prepared for this conundrum – it was not something anyone had talked that openly about, and few books seemed to help answer it honestly, save saying 'don't go there'. I talked with an old Guernsey friend, and decided that anything apart from full-on penetration was probably okay.

Naïve? Out-dated? Some of you reading this will be smiling knowing the dilemma you yourself as a young Christian faced; others of you will be shocked at what you think of as out-dated teachings; others of you will be surprised that I even consented to anything beyond a quick kiss. If there's one thing the Church has handled terribly badly over the years, it's sex.

So, my lines were clear, at least in my mind and I thought in his. I trusted him. We had spent too many hours discussing it all and he was a priest, wasn't he? But despite this, one night it all became just a bit too infuriating for him. He took what was not his to take, my most precious gift which I had not given, and left me with silent tears rolling down my cheeks onto the pillow.

I felt humiliated, ashamed, embarrassed and dirty. I couldn't talk about it – not even to God.

But I knew that He knew, that He had seen and that He would ultimately one day hold people to account.

CHAPTER THREE

Le 'Gai Paris'

November 1991

Following this 'incident', I became increasingly depressed, and my performance plummeted.

There were times when I found myself being completely overwhelmed with sadness, and I struggled to even get out of bed in the mornings. I say I was depressed – I know that now, but I had no idea that that was what I was struggling with at the time. No one did. Mental illness was purely a thing that affected very unstable or very weak people in our society, or so I mistakenly thought.

To be fair, there were additional stresses at work that weren't helping – like a new boss who was a sexist bully. For some inexplicable reason he saw his role as being one that needed to constantly belittle us so as to motivate us to work harder. He would wander nonchalantly into our office, clap his hands and shout: 'Hello, Mushrooms!' and then, when we refused to rise to his bait, he would say: 'Do you know why I call you mushrooms? It's because you live in the dark and feed on shit!' I think he thought it was funny. We didn't – but power has a habit of keeping people quiet, so we put our heads down and endeavoured to make the best of a bad situation.

By the time I came to leave eighteen months later, I was the only female left in our Category Group – all the others had given up and gone. I understand he left the day after me.

He did teach me one very important lesson though, for which I am grateful. It has stayed with me over the years, and I often reflect on it now I'm involved with the hierarchies of the Church.

We were still in the age of faxes, where personal computers were prized machines that we would have to come in over weekends to use. As such, I had taught myself to type and learnt to use a programme called Word. To be honest, I found that typing my own documents was the only way of being able to perfect the one-page memo, which all 'Proctoids' had drummed into them was the only way to communicate.

In November 1991 I was moved from Fairy Liquid to Lenor and given one of the first pan-European briefs. This was a real honour and was a major mark of trust on the company's part in giving me such a senior role so early in my career. I was tasked with co-ordinating the launch of Lenor Ultra across Europe, a revamped version of Lenor Concentrate that aimed to ride the 'ultra' wave that was sweeping through a greener, more environmentally-savvy consumer base. To be honest, the project was doomed from the start; one of the secrets of fabric softener is that evidently homemakers love pouring large quantities into their washing machine – as it represents the time and care they are taking over their loved ones' clothes. We weren't to understand this emotional side of the brand for some time though – being Procter & Gamble, our focus was far too rational. As far as we were concerned we just made their clothing feel softer than everyone else did!

Anyway, with this new position I got my very own computer – quite a status symbol back then.

My secretary therefore had far less typing work to do as a result, and so I used to ask her to help me fax confidential documents to my European colleagues (email was only a dream back then).

One day, needing to answer the phone in our office, my secretary left a very important document on the fax machine situated in the corridor by my boss's office. He happened to pass by, picked up the document and went completely berserk.

Le 'Gai Paris'

Summoning me immediately, he said he was going to fire me. I asked him what I had done, and he waved the fax at me. I was starting to explain that I had no knowledge of what had happened but that I would look into it, when he interrupted me and said – it's your responsibility, I'm holding you totally accountable.

He was right – that's why I was being paid more than my secretary. I needed to be responsible for her actions as well as my own. I apologised and promised it wouldn't happen again, secretly fuming at the injustice of being dragged over the coals for something so relatively minor.

But the lesson was learnt – responsibility and accountability. We must always pay the price for things that are done on our watch by those working for us, even if we weren't aware of them at the time.

The pan-European launch project was fascinating, and resulted in a highly memorable pre-production meeting, which was to go down in marketing history. We had ten different countries involved, and we needed to shoot the ad with ten different voice-overs. I produced flags for every country present and reflected that my dream of joining the Foreign Office had nearly come true.

But I was unhappy – deeply unhappy – and I wanted a change.

I asked if I could move abroad and was told that company policy was that women had to be married to do so. To this day I'm not sure if that was exactly true, but I saw red all the same.

It was enough to make me start looking for another job. I decided that it was time to move out of the corporate sector and into the charity sector, which I had decided would be my best career plan. I had by now learnt some very useful skills, particularly in terms of project management and strategic thinking, and I believed it was time to use them for the greater good.

However, try as I might, the doors just wouldn't open although I did keep being asked to go for an interview with P&G's key competitor, Kimberly-Clark. I was hesitant about this, so I decided to use the fleece approach again.

I lowered my head at my desk and prayed that if I was truly meant to go to this interview, could they possibly ring me within the next ten minutes and offer to fly me down to London – via Guernsey, as I wanted to see my parents – oh, and could they offer double my salary ... I like to make my fleeces really very hard!

The phone started ringing ....

A couple of weeks later I found myself down in Tonbridge at the European Head Office of Kimberly-Clark, having just spent a long weekend in Guernsey. The Category Manager, Clare, had recently left Procter & Gamble and was set on attacking her competition by poaching their best staff. At least that's what she told me on offering me a European Brand Manager position in her division, Feminine Care.

The only slight snag was that one of my great female friends in Newcastle, Jeannie (another member of Jesmond Parish Church), was the brand manager who had just been responsible for the launch of Always into Europe. I realised that this meant that I was going to be working in direct competition to her. I flew back home, took her to one side, and explained that whilst I couldn't say very much from now on we should never meet again in her office, and that she should keep her door locked at all times. Subtle as a brick, but I didn't want her suffering any consequences from the news I was inevitably going to share once the formal offer came through.

As an aside, I must admit this all led to quite a unique speech at her wedding. Having spent a fair bit of her working life in Vienna, Jeanie decided to do things the Austrian way and asked her female friends to offer a couple of speeches during the reception. I therefore stood and talked about her husband having a wonderful 'stay-dry cover' (a complete mansion of a house), and that whilst I thought it might be a challenge to keep her 'firmly fixed in place' he was in fact now offering her a 'new improved' form of security. I remember the relief as one by one the women in the room started to giggle then laugh openly, whilst all the men sat looking around blankly.

Anyway, a few days later I found myself sitting in front of not only my Category Manager (my boss's boss), but also the Company's Legal Secretary. Yes, I may have just resigned – but the trouble was that I was going to the competition, the lead competition. I was given an absolute roasting. I was then marched to my desk to collect my things by a security guard and escorted straight out of the building. What shocked me most however was that on passing one of my colleagues on the stairs, I was spat at. I was stunned – yes, Kimberly-Clark might just have been about to launch a competitor to the brand he worked on, but I knew nothing of this guy's defence plans – and even if I did, I still had my principles and would never have shared them.

But I was viewed as a traitor for switching sides – it was a taste of things to come, I now realise.

———— • ————

The first day of work at any new job is always a bit nerve-racking. You're never too sure who you're going to encounter, what your new team will be like and whether your new post will be all you've been promised it would be.

My first day at Kimberly-Clark was no exception.

I arrived, and immediately sensed things weren't quite what they should be.

People were pleasant enough, but there definitely seemed to be a sense of reserve – even resentment – in the air from many of my new work colleagues. It was only a few months later I was to find out that Clare had not actually got around to telling them that I was starting till the day before I joined, and that unfortunately all my personal details had been found on the office fax machine (what is it with me and fax machines?). This meant that both my age (much younger than the average) and my salary (much higher than the average) had been made known to everyone prior to my arrival – not the best foot on which to start. What's more, there were others in the UK office who felt they should have been allowed to apply for my job.

I soon realised that Clare wasn't that popular and being her first appointment wasn't necessarily a good thing. She had come in and immediately tried to shake things up, which had caused a fair bit of anger amongst those who prided themselves in the fact that Kimberly-Clark was different to Procter & Gamble. She left within a few months, which was both good and bad news for me.

There was something even more memorable about my first day, though, which left me wondering if Jeremy Beadle was going to suddenly appear from behind a pillar with a large microphone and shout 'You've been framed!'. I was informed that I had started on just the right day as the two leading Product Development experts for Feminine Care were over from the United States, and they were going to give us the results of a two-year study they had conducted – involving creatives from a range of professions – into the future of feminine care products.

For the uninitiated this means: sanitary towels, tampons and pantyliners.

I resolved to sit quietly and listen – always a good strategy for one's first day. But after these two gentlemen had proudly set out what a broad range of professions they had drawn their group of experts from, I dared to venture just one question – how many women had been involved in the research? They looked at me quizzically, and asked why did I want to know that? I responded that I thought it was rather self-evident, and they then informed me that about a third were women.

No one, apart from me, seemed surprised by this so I thought it best to wait and see the results.

Le 'Gai Paris'

It was only when we were presented with the two concepts of a 'self-warming tampon' and a 'self-adhesive pad' (meaning that the pad would self-adhere to the body, which would be near-impossible for the vast majority of women who didn't go in for full waxing) that I began to fight back the giggles. I looked around to see if anyone else was finding these ideas as outrageous as I was and realised there appeared to be only one other person in the room who was struggling with it as much as I was – Louise.

What a way to meet a woman who was going to irrevocably change my life.

Evidently, I had been appointed to replace Louise as European Feminine Care Manager for Pantyliners and Tampons, as she was returning to head up Feminine Care in France.

Louise was everything you would expect from a sassy Parisienne. Educated in one of Les Grandes Écoles, she spoke perfect English but with that oh-so-charming slight French accent, that always made me feel that she was deliberately mimicking one of the women from 'Allo 'Allo.

She dressed impeccably, perfecting the smart casual look that the French love, and had a laugh that was so infectious you couldn't help smiling even if you were really frustrated with her.

Louise swiftly became a dear friend, although sadly her time in our office was limited as she was due back in the Paris office as soon as she had completed the 'handover'.

She seemed completely at peace with my appointment, unlike her English counterparts, although she was at pains to explain that my biggest markets in Europe were actually hers, in France, and that things were in a pretty drastic state, with parts of the brand in almost total freefall.

Between us we therefore hatched a plan for me to request to go and spend three months in Paris to review the French business in order to build a European Marketing Strategy that could take into account the core issues that she was facing.

Her PDG (Président-Directeur Général) was completely 'd'accord' with the plan as he too, like most of his continental counterparts, felt that the European Head Office was staffed only by Brits and Americans (which it was) and that hardly any of us understood what it was like over the water, on the Continent (which we didn't).

Clare was dead set against the plan, but once she left my new American boss seemed far more amenable to the idea. To be honest, I think he quite liked having an excuse to travel to Paris on business and recognised that the French Feminine Care business was indeed in dire straits.

———◆◆———

So, I moved to Paris – the day after I had my housewarming party for my first little new house in Pittswood, just outside Hadlow in Kent. I bought this tiny two-bedroom cottage for the grand sum of £68k in 1993. It was the first house the estate agent had shown me, and I couldn't quite believe that I had so easily found 'the one'. As such, I spent another couple of weeks looking around just to make sure but soon realised none compared to this little white-washed cottage.

My move to Tonbridge had also been full of unexpected 'coincidences'.

Given all the heartache I had been through in Newcastle, I decided to take some time out between jobs and arranged to go and visit my uncle and his family in Perth, Australia.

This was going to be a holiday of a lifetime for me, and so I decided I would try to go on and 'do' the whole of the rest of Australia in a couple of weeks. While up in the Daintree Rainforest in Queensland I just happened to meet a couple who lived in Tunbridge Wells (only a few miles south of Tonbridge), who kindly invited me to go and stay with them on my return until I found somewhere more permanent to live. Julian was a lawyer, and a complete God-send when it came to having someone on hand to help me understand the ins and outs of buying a house.

I was beginning to realise how God could connect me with people just when I needed them most.

The weird thing though was that I only got to spend a couple of nights in my new house, but in spite of that it was arguably the best investment I could ever have made.

———•———

I love Paris.

To echo the immortal words of Ella Fitzgerald: *'I love Paris in the Springtime, I love Paris in the Fall…'* I love the language, the cafés, the buildings with their Haussmann architecture, the wide boulevards, the markets and the museums and the shops and the river … and of course the people.

For those of you who know the rest of this song, you'll have realised perhaps just why I fell in love with Paris so much[1] – although it took me a year to work it out, and even then, I had to be told.

———•———

I say I loved Paris, but to be fair the first few months were quite tough.

I was staying in a 'Résidence' (a studio flat in a hotel) in La Défense, a few stops on the RER from our French head office in St Cloud. My schoolgirl French was very rusty and because most members of my team spoke such excellent English, I didn't have that much immediate incentive to learn.

That said, I tried, and would go with Louise to watch French and even Spanish movies (with French subtitles), desperately trying to work out the storyline while allowing the

[1] 'I love Paris, why oh why do I love Paris? Because my love is near …'

barrage of foreign words to wash over me. It was the best way to learn – total immersion – or so I kept being told.

But being surrounded by people speaking French all the time was quite exhausting. My one respite was the English-speaking Anglican church – St Michael's, on the Rue St Honoré.

It was my little oasis of Englishness, and I was quickly roped in by Connie, the music director, to sing and play my violin, which provided me with a readymade set of English and American friends.

This proved invaluable after a nasty incidence towards the end of my third month.

One night after returning home late from seeing the epic new version of Zola's *Germinal* starring Gérard Depardieu, I was stopped by a stranger in the square below my hotel and asked the time. It was past midnight and we were completely alone. I was carrying my violin – made by my father, and arguably the most valuable possession I have ever owned. As I turned my wrist to look at the time, the thickset man pulled out a knife and made to cut off my handbag strap from my arm. Startled and petrified I let it drop to the floor. He grabbed it and ran.

I remember stumbling over to the reception, shaking, and trying to explain to them in my pidgin French what had happened. Stopping the credit cards was easy enough, it was the loss of my address book with all my friends' contact details that really upset me, along with my reading glasses and my favourite pen. All I could think about though was how fortunate I was that he hadn't realised the value of my violin – in fact, I doubt he realised what I was carrying at all.

The thing that scared me most, though, was that he now had the key card to my 'Résidence', and so I demanded to move somewhere else immediately. For some reason the hotel couldn't accommodate this at such short notice, and so I ended up sleeping on Connie's (the music director from St Michael's) sofa bed for a few nights until the office got a new hotel sorted out.

I realise now I got off very lightly. A year or so later I read an article in a French magazine about a serial rapist who had attacked women in La Défense. I turned to the article and froze when I saw the man's photograph. Things could have indeed been far, far worse.

———•———

As with all things, God somehow worked everything together for good, as I was about to find out.

At the end of my initial three-month period I presented my analysis and recommendations to my American boss and his boss, who had both decided to come over for the day. I explained that the French business was in significant difficulty. It was so bad, I surmised, that they should in fact cut their losses and consider closing it down (sorry, Louise). I argued that they had neither the products, the promotional budget nor the personnel to pull off the great u-turn that was needed.

The two men looked at each other, smiled, and then suggested something that I was totally unprepared for. Would I be interested in moving to France and being the 'personnel' I had identified, if they promised to give me both the 'products' and the 'promotional budget'?

It took me a split second to decide – another few years in Paris? Er, now let me think about that for a second … *Mais oui! Bien sur! Ça sera avec grand plaisir!*

So, I got to stay in Paris!

It was just before Christmas, and I had exactly two days to find an apartment that I could move into on my return from the Christmas break. I dropped everything and spent two of the most depressing days of my time out there viewing some of the worst accommodation I have ever seen. The French don't tend to rent apartments 'fully furnished', and now I could see why.

Closing the door on the last flat I began to think I had made a terrible mistake. Perhaps it was best to go back to England after all. I decided to pop back into the office and contact my boss to explain the situation. However, on arriving at my desk I saw a large yellow post-it note on my phone saying, 'Ring Connie – urgent'. Given the kindness she had shown me, I wasted no time in calling her back – fearing that something awful might have happened to her.

She answered immediately, and asked me if I was still looking for a flat? Confused, I said yes, I was – although I had more or less given up on finding one before Christmas.

'Good', she said, 'can you get to the Rue St Honoré within the hour?' It turned out that a close friend of hers, Carole, had just been let down at the last minute by a guy who was supposed to be renting her flat that evening. She was leaving for England first thing in the morning and was keen to meet me, and – if I liked the flat – give me a set of keys.

'Why has he pulled out?' I asked. 'Oh, something to do with the fact his girlfriend didn't like the idea of the flat being on the sixth floor without a lift!'

Lift or no lift, Carole's flat was absolutely *fabulous*!

As I was to learn, Carole had for many years headed up restoration at Le Louvre – a building which just happened to be visible from her balcony. As such her home was her own mini-art gallery of restored works, and she therefore wanted someone she could trust to look after it. With a balcony onto the road and a mezzanine level with a bedroom and bathroom, this was by far the most stunning flat I had ever set foot in in Paris. The main wall of the living room stretched high up into the rafters and was covered from top to bottom with countless works of art.

Getting there was not half as difficult as it had been made out to be – one first climbed a spiral staircase up a few levels to a little iron bridge and then there were three more flights up a sixteenth-century staircase. It all felt like an old-style French version of *Alice in Wonderland*.

I pinched myself – I just couldn't believe my luck. Someone was definitely looking after me.

Le 'Gai Paris'

And so, I came to live in Paris – a city where for the first time in my life I felt I could be truly free to be me. No one knew me. No one had any expectations of me. No one was trying to box me in.

I could be whoever I wanted to be – the question for me though was, who exactly *was* that?

Louise and I devoted ourselves to turning the business round. We worked quite literally day and night, stopping just to eat and drink, or – if it was the end of the week – see a movie.

I loved being in her company. We worked so well together, helped by the fact we had the same sense of humour and the same core values. We were equally motivated, equally determined, and had an equal dislike of the European Head Office who 'just didn't get the continental markets'.

Looking back now I realise I perhaps should have seen the warning signs of what was happening when I agreed to do something that was so far out of my character type, it was laughable.

In order to relaunch the brand, we had pulled in every favour we could muster with the French Sales team and our IT department. We had been lent the first prototype of something called a 'tablet' on which we had loaded a couple of power-point presentations and a film we had made 'expres'. This included a truly remarkable product demonstration by the leading independent product tester in Europe, showing how our products were superior to those of the competition.

Time was short, and we had literally days before we were meant to relaunch the brand to the French trade. The only snag was that we had both been summoned to a European Feminine Care meeting over in Tonbridge, and neither of us really had the time to go.

So, I agreed to do something for Louise that to this day I can't believe I did. I lied. Not just a small white lie, but a big fat hairy lie. It was something so outrageously stupid that even now I can't think what brought me to do it. (Well, I suppose I can, but that would be giving the game away.)

Up until the night before we were meant to fly to Gatwick I still wasn't sure whether I would go through with the plan or not. I vividly remember waking, looking at my alarm clock, and thinking for a split second that I could still make the flight. But then I turned over and that was that. My heart was pounding. I called Louise who, laughing, said: 'Okay, we're going through with it then!'

And the 'it'?

Wait for it … I was to feign a heart attack!

Yep, it was that dramatic. Evidently, I had woken feeling ill (which was more or less true, given how churned up I was over all this), felt sharp pains down my left-hand side (which I had had only a few months before, and had been tested for) and Louise had therefore taken me into hospital.

Her brother was a doctor, and so she therefore knew which hospital she should theoretically be taking me to. I hadn't got a clue. She came over to the flat and we … worked.

As I think about it now, the funniest thing about this surreal episode is that I risked jeopardising my career and my reputation for the sake of some sanitary products. Most people 'throw a sicky' to go off on a long weekend or spend time with a lover … I was doing it to save my brand!

Oh, and to be with Louise of course.

Somehow, we pulled it off. I took a few days off work to make it all seem real, while all the time working on our launch presentation. On returning to the office, however, I had to remember to take things slowly and more importantly to ensure that I had the same story as Louise.

Le 'Gai Paris'

It was shortly after this that Louise's best friend, Béatrice, asked me out for dinner.

I liked Béatrice – she was a real character. A strong, independent, forthright French woman with class. She loved colour and would somehow manage to get away with mixing oranges and reds and greens and purples in ways that we English would never have dared.

I can't remember how we actually first met – I assume at a supper with Louise one night. However it had been, we soon became good friends in our own right, which was to be a great blessing to me.

This particular evening, though, I know we had only just started to get to know each other.

She had suggested quite an expensive restaurant, which I was happy to try. We ordered a good bottle of Bordeaux, which I remember relishing – in fact I think we might have even ordered a second. What I do recall is that once the main course was over, we went straight to coffee.

It was at this point that Béatrice looked at me and in her thick French-accented English said: 'Now, Jayne, when are you going to admit that you are madly in love with Louise?'

In shock, I reached out for my glass, and instead managed to knock it over. The deep ruby red liquid spilt all over the starched white table cloth and started to seep down the sides of the table. It felt like my very insides were spilling out – and well they might have been.

I looked at her astonished – what on earth did she mean? She smiled, and continued gently: 'But, Jayne, it's so obvious to everyone it seems, but you!'

She was right of course.

The only person who hadn't been able to see the

bleeding obvious for the past year was me – and, I hoped, Louise.

———•◦•———

I went home with my head racing. What on earth was I going to do? Was it true? Was she right? Could a woman love another woman? What on earth did that actually *mean*?

And most of all – was it reciprocated?

———•◦•———

Ironically at that time it didn't cross my mind to ask what God might think about it, I was too wrapped up trying to work out how I myself felt about it all.

———•◦•———

I decided that the best thing to do was to talk to Louise. If it had been so obvious to Béatrice, maybe she too was aware and was just waiting for me to say something?

We had by now relaunched the brand, and things were going well – sales were even starting to pick up. I was due to go around to her house for supper later that week and decided that this would be the ideal time and place to talk privately about it.

I must admit my mind was all over the place. I had no idea whether acting on my feelings would bring the happiness I so desperately craved, but I recognised the truth about the fact I absolutely loved being with Louise, and that my world lit up every time she walked into the room.

The question you're probably asking though is, what about any physical desire? I would have to be honest and say that I was so utterly closed down in that department, the thought hadn't even crossed my mind. It was romantic love that I sought, not sex.

Le 'Gai Paris'

So, I decided to talk to her, in French. Bad move. It led to one of the most awkward exchanges I think I've ever had in my life, which went something along the following lines:

'*Louise, j'ai quelque choses de très important a te dire* (I've something very important to tell you)....'

I paused as she looked up from pouring the coffee.

'*Je t'aime, Louise.*'

'*Quoi?* (what?)' she said shaking her head, '*Non, non, non, Jayne, tu voulais dire "Je t'aime beaucoup!"* (what you meant to say is that I like you very much – as a good friend).'

Definitely lost in translation.

I assured her that my French was correct, and switched to English, and repeated it.

I remember the look of horror on her face – that's about all really, the rest is a bit of a blank.

Sadly, Louise never really spoke to me again.

She applied to move to manage the Own Label brands and at the same time I was promoted into her place as Head of French Feminine Care. This was quite a coup as I was the first non-national to be appointed to such a role. I should have been over the moon, especially as it meant I was now going to be staying in France permanently, but I was mortified – and of course heartbroken.

People must have recognised something was drastically wrong, as we suddenly were no longer spending any time together. But nobody said anything – well not to me anyway.

I looked for a way out, and fortunately saw a notice by the coffee machine one morning (note, a *real* coffee machine that did double expressos in small cups) asking for applications to join a small select group that would be tasked with launching Kimberly-Clark into Central and Eastern Europe.

It was to be led by the then Vice President of Europe, Tony Harris, who had decided he wanted a change of role, although he had also decided that he would remain in his office in Paris. The other thing he got to keep was the business use of the

Just Love

Kimberly-Clark company jet! I applied and was immediately appointed. The only slight problem was that it meant I had to take over Louise's office as it was nearer Tony's ... and she was asked to move downstairs. I know she must have felt this was adding insult to injury, but I truly didn't have any choice in the matter.

CHAPTER FOUR

From Russia with Love

October 1994

My new role focusing on Central and Eastern Europe was fascinating – although we were hopelessly naive. What's more we were one of the last major multi-national FMCG[1] companies to enter the region, which was then reeling from the amount of foreign investment it was attracting.

I remember Tony hosting our first 'Central and Eastern Group' meeting in the boardroom with me, David (a senior Director of Finance, who wanted a new challenge before he retired) and Bert (a senior Dutch Sales Director, who like David wanted one final challenge). Bert, David and I became firm friends – which was just as well given the amount of travelling we had to do together. To be honest, I think I probably spent more time with them over the next two years than their wives did. They were extremely good to me though, and I learnt a huge amount from them both.

Anyway, in our first meeting Tony looked at us all and asked whether any of us had ever been to Central and Eastern Europe? No – this was 1993 and the big blank block to the east of West Germany was still unfamiliar territory to most. He then asked whether we knew the capitals of any of the key countries we were meant to be dealing with. I hazarded a few guesses and performed a bit better than the other two.

[1] Fast-moving consumer goods companies

Absolutely unbelievable when I think about it now.

I was tasked with trying to understand the nature of the differing markets we wanted to enter, which included drawing up consumer profiles of the types of consumers we would be marketing to. Given there were virtually no research companies operating in these countries yet, I decided my best strategy was to work with our advertising agency, Ogilvy & Mather (O&M), who had recently opened offices in our priority countries – Hungary, the Czech Republic, Poland and Russia.

Our priority was of course Russia – the biggest and yet most dangerous (as we were to learn) market of all. I soon realised that we were at a severe disadvantage being so behind the likes of Unilever and Procter & Gamble, who had already established their offices and were fast making headway into these lucrative consumer bases. We therefore needed a different strategy that would enable us to penetrate the markets quickly – so we focused on buying up well-known local companies (and their brands), injecting new technology, and then using their well-established sales and distribution networks to ensure we could get our products to market quickly.

I booked to travel out to Moscow for four days to work with our O&M Client Manager, Tatjana.

Nothing could have prepared me for what I was to experience out there.

My overwhelming memory was the cold – I have never experienced temperatures like it. I thought my ears were literally about to snap off, so much so that hats were a necessity, not a fashion item. Then there was the extreme poverty – with old ladies selling anything they could, including their husbands' socks, to buy bread. And then, right alongside it all, there was the affluence.

The latter hit me from the start. On my first night at the Hotel Metropole I remember a man at the restaurant table next to me who had a briefcase that was fastened with a long silver chain to his wrist. I watched with intrigue as, on being presented with the bill, he opened it and pulled out a stack of dollars. Peering across I could see that his briefcase was packed full of these tightly bound wads of green paper. At nearly $50 for some salmon linguine, I could see why.

Tatjana – who I had yet to meet – had been tasked with 'introducing me to Russia', and I was down to meet her at 10 o'clock the next morning in the hotel lobby.

After a terrible night's sleep in my tiny cell of a room, which somehow cost two hundred dollars a night, I found myself sitting in reception and listening to the resident harpist. I remember thinking that this was quite some way of starting the day, and then watched as a tall, elegant blond in a fur coat glided in and looked around. She seemed straight out of a movie. Seeing me, she smiled and walked over with her hand outstretched. 'Hello, Gee-ayne', she said in a thick Russian accent, which put added emphasis on the 'J'. I was utterly mesmerised.

It was arguably the most eye-opening trip of my life. We were driven around the city by her personal driver (who I later learnt was also her bodyguard), who spoke absolutely no English. He had a 4x4 jeep, which was obviously quite a status symbol, and kept his semi-automatic clearly on show in the open glove compartment. I looked at it in alarm, which elicited the following response from Tatjana, her sharp facial features working overtime: 'Don't worry, Gee-ayne. Everyone carries one. The windows are blacked out – just like the mafia – no one will look in or stop us.'

She had decided that, as a Westerner working for a large multi-national, I must be extremely rich and so suggested we spent my first morning in the GUM – an imposing building housing all the major international shops, which only foreigners were allowed in to. Our first store, much to my horror, was a shop selling mink coats. I remember her calling me over to feel how soft one particular coat was and, after seeing me nod in agreement, she smiled and said 'This is the baby mink, Gee-ayne, by far the best!'. I knew I needed to get out and so explained that this wasn't really the type of 'store checking' I had in mind. Seeing her confusion, I told her that what I really needed was to go to places which sold paper products like tissues, sanitary towels, toilet paper and if possible, nappies. I remember her looking at me quizzically as I tried to explain that that was why I was here – to learn what people bought, and how much they were prepared to spend.

I then began to see real Russian life – we tried numerous stores, from open market stores to small corner shops, which had virtually no products in them at all. Tatjana explained that people would shout whenever they saw a delivery lorry approaching, and that everyone would then rush to form a queue in order to see if there was anything they could buy. It was an education into the difficulties of post-Soviet Russia, where distribution was still a very significant problem.

That evening we went to the Bolshoi, and I had my very first experience of opera – *Tosca*. It was surreal. Here I was with this extraordinary woman, sitting in an opera hall that used to be filled with first white Russians and then communists. At the interval she asked if I wanted a drink, and I suggested a gin and tonic would be very welcome. We went off to the bar, where I was presented with a glass of gin and a glass of tonic – in equal measures. I couldn't help smiling. Seeing this Tatjana explained that they did it like that so that the customer could see how much gin they were being served.

The next day our driver came to pick me up. He smiled and started making some jokes – in Russian. I mentioned this to Tatjana when I got to the office. 'Oh, you are family now', she explained. 'He thinks you're okay. He'll take a bullet for you!' She must have seen the look on my face, and so took me by the arm and walked me outside. We got back into the car, and she instructed our driver to 'just drive'. She then proceeded to tell me her life story, well, the critical parts of it anyway.

She had been married to a colonel in the army – evidently a very senior army colonel. Although she must have been just

From Russia with Love

a few years older than me, I got the impression that he was much older than her. He had been arrested some years before, I forget now whether it was during the Gorbachev or Yeltsin eras – but the key thing was that she had escaped, out of the back door of the house, with a couple of jewels that he had given her. She was obviously 'high class Russian' and a target, and so her 'driver' – who she employed – was sworn to look after her, and those close to her.

It sounded like a story out of a thriller. If it wasn't for her obvious charisma and sheer elegance and charm I would never have believed her. But I could see from her eyes that she was obviously telling the truth, and moreover she had no idea about what had happened to her husband.

I think she also knew the effect she had on me.

She would reach over and tap my hand whenever she wanted to say something, and whisper in my ear, letting hair fall and touch my face: 'You zee, Gee-ayne, it's like zis ….'

I had no idea what to do or say. I just let a host of feelings sweep over me – and put it down to my being in a foreign country and being escorted by a beautiful foreign princess of a woman.

For our last night I offered to take both her and her driver out for a meal. She smiled and began chatting to her driver. A few minutes later she turned to me and said that he wanted to go to McDonalds. I started to protest and explained that I wanted to take him out for a 'proper' meal, to which she began to laugh. McDonalds *was* a proper meal – in fact it was where *everyone* in Moscow wanted to go as it had just opened. We agreed that he would drop us off at a restaurant she knew en route, and that once he'd had his Big Mac, he would come and take us home.

The next day the two of them drove me to the airport. I can still smell her expensive perfume as she embraced me, kissing me firmly on both cheeks. 'Come back and zee us zoon, Gee-ayne!'

Just Love

I wish I could have, Tatjana – if you're still out there, I'd love to hear from you.

———•◆•———

Those years working in Central and Eastern Europe were some of the most formative in my career.

I worked on mergers and acquisitions, listened in on boardroom deals, and learnt how different each of our Eastern European neighbours are – and how similar. I also had a baptism of fire into the realities of conducting business in countries which did not always operate under the same rule of law.

We decided that given the amount of vodka that needed to be drunk in cementing business deals in Russia, it was no place for a woman – and after having experienced this first hand, I agreed.

In retrospect, we were extremely lucky given our naivety. I remember remarking once to Tony as we disembarked from our private jet into two waiting blacked-out Mercedes 'that we looked like the mafia'. Pointing at each of us in turn, I explained we had the boss (Tony), his bodyguard (Bert), his banker (David) and his floozy (me!). (Certainly, the hotel receptionist seemed to think so, when later that day she checked both Tony and I into the same room.) We had then sped off into the frozen tundra of the countryside and after an hour in silence I asked Tony quietly how did we know if we were going in the right direction. Abductions of business men and women were on the increase at the time, and I was rather scared. His answer didn't help – he admitted he had no idea, and that we would just have to sit it out and wait. It was the longest two hours of my life.

Around the same time an old university friend, Amanda Norman, turned up at St Michael's church. I remember spotting her one Sunday in the congregation and asking her what she was doing in Paris – she went slightly red and introduced me to her new husband, Andrew, who was in fact being interviewed as our new assistant vicar. He was duly appointed, which was great news for all of us, especially Amanda and I, as it meant we both had an 'old friend' in who we could confide.

Whilst I didn't feel able to talk to her about my myriad of feelings surrounding Louise and Tatjana, I was able to share with her about the growing unease I had working for a multinational that was considering closing-down a large factory in Wales – and so laying off dozens of workers – in order to move production to a cheaper base in the Czech Republic. My conscience was being pricked in more than one way, and I wasn't too sure how long I felt I could continue working at Kimberly-Clark.

Amanda encouraged me to go on the St Michael's House party so that I could have a break from it all. It would also provide an opportunity to pray about what I should be doing next. I was slightly nervous still about being in an intense Christian environment, the ghost of Guernsey still weighing large on me, but I decided that it would at least give me a fun break and some space to reflect.

It was during this long weekend that I had an overwhelming sense that it was time for me to return home to England. I couldn't articulate why, but I just 'knew' that my present chapter was coming to an end, and that I needed to be ready to face whatever was coming next.

I remember driving back to Paris later that evening and wondering how on earth I was going to find a job back in the UK when I was still stuck in France?

The answer was far simpler than I could ever have imagined. The next morning the phone rang, and a head-hunter asked if I might be interested in meeting a client of his who was keen to talk to me about setting up a new marketing division as they wanted to become more consumer focused.

The client just happened to be BBC Television.

I remember laughing and saying that I thought I was arguably the last person they should want to meet – I didn't own a television and hadn't watched the BBC for the past three years.

Nevertheless, I agreed to go to interview, and we set a date.

The only problem was that the date coincided with a major tube strike in France, which made getting to the airport almost impossible. I arrived over an hour late and ran straight to the gate to be told I had missed my flight by 5 minutes. Being a BA Gold Card holder (the one perk I must admit I still miss) they agreed to put me on the next flight, which was due to leave shortly.

With some relief I boarded the plane and took my seat in the middle of the plane. We taxied down the apron towards the runaway and then came suddenly to an abrupt stop. The pilot announced that the plane in front – the one I had originally been due to take – had had a severe technical fault (its tyres had burst as it was about to take off) and that we were going to have to wait a while for the runway to be cleared. I froze – how on earth was I going to let anyone know that I was late?

After an hour on the apron, I went to see the air hostess and explained my situation. I was about to have an important interview and was there any way at all that we could get a message to the ground staff to ask them to let someone know. It was a long chance I knew, but I was really concerned that being late wasn't going to put me in the best of lights. The hostess kindly spoke to the pilot, who explained he couldn't do much, but said he had requested a member of the ground staff to be at the gate with a mobile phone (they were very rare back then) for me to call the BBC.

We eventually took off and landed at Heathrow, but because we were so late the usual gate was not available to us. I was moved up to the front of the plane (it is amazing what a Gold Card can do) and was assured I would be first off. After yet more waiting, the captain came onto the tannoy and said that sadly there was a problem with the mechanics of the gate, and that we were going to have to disembark from the back of the plane. At this point I just started to laugh, and thought 'Okay, Mr God, I get it, I'm either definitely not meant to get this job, or I most definitely am!'

My original plan had been to go to my sister's, who was at this stage studying medicine at Charing Cross hospital, to get changed. Time was now of the essence, so I jumped in a black cab and asked the driver if he minded if I got changed as we drove. I seem to remember that the hardest thing was trying to pull up my tights without attracting too much attention from passing cars.

Finally, we got to BBC Television Centre in Shepherd's Bush and I rushed up to Pam Masters' office, my potential new boss and the Controller of Broadcasting and Presentation. I had just reached her outer office and was about to offer profuse apologies to her secretary for being so late, when Pam herself came out, shook my hand and apologised for over-running. I had literally arrived at the perfect time! In somewhat of a stupor I went into the interview, knowing that this was obviously 'meant to be', and accepted the post that was offered shortly afterwards.

The only slight problem was that I hadn't really grasped what the job was actually all about, but I thought that was just academic and that I'd work it out in time. The Job Description had been worded with lots of internal BBC jargon, which hadn't made too much sense to an outsider like myself. I knew it was to do with marketing, strategy and television – which sounded both fun and interesting. However, I had come to think that this meant I was going to be selling programmes like *Fawlty Towers* to the Americans. It therefore did come as a bit of a surprise to me when I found myself overseeing all the trailing time between the programmes, and the formulation of branding strategies for all the BBC terrestrial, satellite and new digital TV channels.

I went back to Paris, and realised I was going to have to find a way of breaking the news to Tony.

Just Love

I decided the best thing was to tell him as soon as I could – so I went in early the next Monday morning, popped my head around his door and asked if I could have a word.

He nodded and said he was glad to see me as he had some important news he needed to share. I grabbed us both coffees, took a deep breath and went in. Before I had even sat down he started to explain that he had finally had the results of some research he had commissioned a few months earlier to look at where the optimal base should be for our new Central and Eastern European venture. The results clearly indicated that we needed to relocate to Vienna. He stopped to see the impact that this (supposedly very welcome) news would have – as he knew full well that the one place I'd always said I wanted to move to, given a choice, was Vienna.

I felt winded. It was true – I had dreamt of living in Vienna, and if there was one thing I might have considered over the BBC it would have been that. However, deep down I 'knew' I was meant to go back to London, even if this was in fact the very last place I wanted to live. This sense of 'knowing' was something that was getting stronger, I could never explain it, it just always 'was'.

Tony was rather unhappy to say the least when I told him my news. He took it as a personal slight that I didn't want to stay with the company and decided that as a punishment he would make me work my whole notice. I have always thought making someone do this is counter-productive – I mean, why would you ever want someone working for you who quite obviously doesn't want to be there, isn't motivated and has no desire to ensure that things are done properly? Of course, he knew me better than that, and knew that I would keep my standards, but I was angry that I had to commute for two months between Notting Hill and Maidstone – a two-hour journey each way.

From Russia with Love

In February 1996 I started as the new Head of Marketing for BBC Television, based in BBC Television Centre. It was an extraordinary job – working alongside the Channel Controllers, which meant Alan Yentob and Michael Jackson, and then later Mark Thompson. My role was to devise a strategy to optimise the use of our promotional airtime, while also helping to devise a more marketing-centred approach to television. These were the days of John Birt, who wanted to transform television to make it a more viewer-centric (rather than producer-centric) business. The only problem was that the rest of the BBC didn't see things in quite the same way, and the addition onto the team of a young new marketing guru (who had still to reach her thirtieth birthday and who'd never worked in television before) wasn't exactly their idea of progress.

I had a very steep learning curve, and one that would prove invaluable in years to come when dealing with another organisation managed primarily by men who found having a young marketing woman on their team a little out of the ordinary.

The good news was that I had a complete champion in my new boss, Pam, who was known as the 'Silent Queen of Television'. She had launched Channel 4 and was married to Alan Boyd of Grundig (and *Blind Date*) fame. They were a formidable couple, and I realised in many ways I was being presented as her new prodigy. She had worked relentlessly over the years to develop the BBC brand with Martin Lambie-Nairn and had just introduced the new BBC2 idents when I joined.

She knew things weren't easy for me, and that I had nearly every TV producer within Television Centre on my back wanting me to promote their programme over everyone else's. This meant she was open to me making a rather unusual request, just weeks after joining.

The truth was that as I was about to leave Kimberly-Clark I'd had a letter from British Airways to say that I had succeeded in a members' only promotion that I hadn't even realised I'd been entered into. (I think I had my secretary to thank for that.) It seems I had travelled enough business class flights during the last month to have been awarded a return flight on Concorde!

With hindsight, given the demise of Concorde, I rather wish I had taken the prize just as it was.

But at the time, believing I was at the start of my international career, and feeling that I could in fact go to New York at any time I wanted, I rang and asked whether I could change it for something else? They suggested a First Class return ticket to anywhere in the world (which should have given me an idea how valuable the Concorde ticket was). I thought this sounded a much better deal and asked whether I could go to Cairns in Australia via a few choice places en route. They seemed quite happy with this – all I needed was to convince my new boss that she wanted to give me a five-week holiday within a few months of me starting!

I asked to see Pam and explained to her the wonderful news I had been given about the free flight. I remember her looking at me over her glasses and saying, 'Well, Jayne, if that was me I'd want to take a good month or two off.' I could have hugged her – she really did get it!

————◆————

So that's how I came to be on a live-aboard on the Great Barrier Reef for a two-week scuba diving holiday. I had saved the money I would have spent on a flight and splashed out on this diving trip.

It was a bit of a risk of course – two weeks on a boat with ten other people (and as we were to find two children – which wasn't allowed according to the brochure) can be hell if folk don't get on.

But luckily, we did. I mean, we *really* did!

I was a little nervous about the trip to say the least, as I'd only just got my scuba diving qualifications and I knew there were going to be some seriously taxing dives. However, I knew it was going to be an adventure too, and I was sure I'd meet some interesting people.

I arrived at the harbour in Cairns and tried to find the boat. A bronzed bearded man came up to me and asked if I was Jayne, and then introduced himself as Pete, our captain. He explained that there was in fact a small technical problem with the boat we had originally chartered and that we would instead be changing boats to a much nicer, but smaller, boat. The knock-on effect of this was that, sadly, I was not going to get my own cabin but would in fact need to share. I must admit to not being very happy about this at all – it wasn't what I had paid for, and I didn't like the idea of sharing with someone I didn't know. He understood, and took me off to see the two boats. I began to appreciate that even if our new one was smaller, it was indeed a far better boat (in fact, it turned out to be his own private boat). So, the question now was, would I rather share with the other single male diver, called Ray, or would I mind sharing with the onboard chef, Rebecca?

It was a no brainer – Rebecca of course.

The cabins were tiny and airless – they were purely for sleeping, although being right next to the engine I couldn't quite work out how that was going to easily happen. Two nights in and six dives down though and I was sleeping like a log.

The only thing left was for me to meet Rebecca ….

Oh … My … Goodness!

The moment I saw her climb aboard I realised I was going to have an eventful few weeks. This Austrian brunette, who oozed sex, charm and confidence was, I realised, far more than just a chef. She had previously worked on the big Marlin Fishing boats, and was now 'living her dream' and spending her time doing the things she loved.

The first day I tried to avoid her – memories of Tatjana and Louise too raw in my head. I thought that that had just been a 'phase', and ones best left in Paris and Moscow. I had come back to England to get on with my life, to settle down and hopefully find the right man.

And now this.

Our first dive was at the world-renowned Cod Hole, famous for its giant potato cod – which are over 8ft long and weigh around 110kg. It was a memorable way to start the trip.

We suited up and Captain Pete gave us our dive briefing. I tried to listen in as much as I could, but my head was all over the place and I was nervous – especially given how few diving hours I had under my belt. The one word which stood out though, which I had not heard before and which he kept using was 'pelagic'. This was to be an excellent 'pelagic dive' with lots of 'pelagic activity'.

I snuck off to ask the one person I thought I could trust and who wasn't diving.

'What does pelagic mean, Rebecca?'

'Seriously? You've not heard of the term "pelagic" before?' she grinned, and her perfect white teeth seemed to take over her face.

'No, afraid not. Is it Australian for something?'

'Boy, you're in for a treat then ... it means ... *shark*!'

Evidently, I went completely white and very quiet. Rebecca, seeing my reaction, went off to find Peter, who had originally suggested I dive in a group of three (which isn't that standard practice), and told him that she thought it would be better if I had my own dive buddy. Realising how new I was to scuba diving, he agreed and said he'd be more than happy to buddy up with me himself. I was so grateful – I didn't want to miss out on the dive, but I had to admit I was petrified.

The first thing that struck me on the dive was how clear the water was, you could see for literally miles. However, at the first sign of sharks – and there was a lot of them – I grabbed hold of Pete's arm. He smiled with his eyes (you can't say too much with a mask) and took my hand. We continued the dive like that. On surfacing, I realised I had bitten through my mouthpiece in sheer terror – the gum guards were chewed straight off. It's still on my mantelpiece as a reminder.

———•———

Those fourteen days on board that boat were, without doubt, some of the happiest days I had lived up till then. Miles away from anywhere and anyone, it was just our little world.

Ray (the single male gay diver), Rebecca and I would lounge out on the large blue mat that covered the front of the boat, lying in a mass of arms and legs as we tried to find ways of ensuring we were making the most of the sun. We told stories, we laughed, we cried, we teased, we laughed again. I adored those times together – it was heaven on earth.

Nothing was ever said, but I assumed Rebecca knew how completely smitten I was with her.

On our last night back in Cairns, she suggested that she 'showed me the town' and introduced me to her friends. She booked a hotel room for me near the airport, which I think belonged to some friends of hers, and I spent the evening wondering if she was coming back with me or not.

The best solution was to get drunk – something we hadn't done on the boat because alcohol doesn't mix well with diving, it's far too dangerous.

She did come back with me to the hotel – she wanted to make sure I got on the plane she said.

Lying next to her in bed, I wondered what on earth I was doing there and whether she was feeling what I was feeling. It was arguably one of the most challenging situations I've ever had to endure.

I had no idea what I wanted – I couldn't name it, I couldn't say it. I suppose I just wanted to touch her, not sexually, that was way too far for me – I just wanted to touch her skin and hold her.

I summoned all my courage – and tried to say as much. The words came out in a jumble. Perhaps it was easier speaking French after all. She understood what I was trying to say though, and just shook her head.

I was mortified. Rejection again.

———•———

The next day I got the plane home and decided I had to draw a line under all this.

Enough was enough – what on earth was I playing at?

I put it down to being in exotic places with exotic women – France, Russia, Australia.

A spell back in London would definitely sort me out!

CHAPTER FIVE

In the Chair

May 1997

'I think you should change your religion, Jayne.'

I looked intently at my psychiatrist to see if she was joking, and realised she was speaking in earnest. This was my first appointment and I wasn't finding it very easy, in fact I wasn't finding *her* very easy. She had come highly recommended by my GP, who had urged me to see her as she thought it would do me good to 'talk to someone'. We were sitting in her rather austere office at the Priory Hospital in Roehampton, which I couldn't help thinking reflected her personality perfectly. Although sitting just a few feet apart, a major chasm had now opened up between us.

'She really doesn't get it', I thought.

Why, oh why had I risked telling her the one thing that had been screaming around my mind ever since my return home from Australia? It had kept me awake for endless nights and had driven me to such a point of stress that I'd been admitted to the Cromwell Hospital with severe but undiagnosed abdominal pain. I hadn't felt able to tell anyone else, least of all my friends from church, for fear of being boxed and put on the eternal 'unsound' step. However, this now seemed far worse.

Change my religion? I could no more do that than I could stop breathing. Jesus wasn't an optional extra that I had decided to pick off the shelf one day. He was as real to me as she was sitting next to me. I hesitated to tell her that, though, as I feared she'd add it to my list of complaints.

So, I bit my lip and decided it was best never to mention 'it' ever again.

My struggle between my faith and my sexuality would have to be a very private affair.

———— • ————

The previous nine months had been some of the darkest in my life, although to be fair there had also been moments of great light too.

Following my return from Australia I had decided it was time I 'settled down' and tried to form some sort of 'ordinary' life. So, I had joined the Kensington Symphony Orchestra, thanks to a BBC friend, Diana, whose fiancé was the main conductor. I also started attending St Paul's Onslow Square, whose claim to fame was that it had originally planted Holy Trinity Brompton since both were in the same parish. I had originally chosen to go to St Paul's as it was where some old friends from Cambridge worshipped, although I was still highly sceptical of anything charismatic.

Both decisions had borne fruit in their own way.

At my first orchestral rehearsal I had been asked to sit on the front desk so that the leader could work out where I should sit in the violin desk 'pecking order'. The rehearsal just happened to be being taken by a guest conductor whose eyes I kept meeting given I automatically (and with some embarrassment) kept sliding back into my old familiar role as leader[1]. I suppose it was quite romantic really. I certainly liked his smile, and his passion for the music. After the rehearsal he introduced himself and asked if I'd like to join everyone for a drink afterwards. I remember thinking how kind it was of him to make me feel so welcome.

[1] The rapport between conductor and leader is critical in any orchestra, as it sets the tone for the rest of the orchestra.

In the Chair

On arriving home later that evening I got an excited phone call from my friend, Diana, who said that he, Geoff, had rung to ask her for my phone number, and would I like her to give it to him? I explained I was a bit confused because he had spent the evening talking about his wife.

'Oh no,' she said, 'is he still doing that? It's so sad. His wife died of cancer a year or so ago, and he's still in the habit of talking about her in the present tense. But you've really made quite an impression on him, Jayne, and it's brilliant he's so keen to ask you out!'

Ask me out?!

I realised I was twenty-eight years old and I had never been asked out before. What's more, I didn't know what the 'rules of the game' were and managed to say as much to Diana. She roared with laughter and said 'well, whatever you feel like', but then caught herself and said: 'Look, Jayne, we've been hoping Geoff would meet someone for some time now, and it's great it's you – the four of us can do so much together!'

It certainly did seem a coincidence that one of my friends was engaged to a chap whose best friend just happened to be my potential new boyfriend.

Geoff called, and we arranged to meet later that week.

I was on cloud nine. I remember riding the tube and looking at all the couples sitting together thinking – that's going to be me!

I was also nervous as hell.

We had a lovely first date. Supper in South Kensington and a walk – hand in hand – around the neat tree-lined residential areas that make up one of the richer postcodes of London.

Geoff was a real gentleman, and so easy to talk to – and laugh with.

I realised we were both fairly nervous, although we dealt

with it in differing ways – I, through having a glass or two of wine, Geoff, through talking non-stop (he didn't drink).

We agreed to meet again, and then again.

On our third date I felt it was time to 'have the conversation', which basically meant I needed to spell out to him that I was committed Christian and that I didn't believe in sex before marriage. I thought that would be enough to put any man off, but no, not Geoff. He just took my hand and said he understood, that he respected my wishes and that that wasn't the primary reason for dating me anyway – he just loved being with me and wanted us to be able to build on that. The look of utter relief must have shown on my face as he reached over and gave me a gentle kiss.

As I say, Geoff was a complete gentleman.

I say that even if, in his own words, he was a 'loud Aussie'. He was a professional double bass player, who also taught the cello. His real love was conducting, for which he harboured a dream of conducting the 'Rite of Spring' at the Royal Festival Hall. His wife, whom he had loved very much, had been quite a famous singer. She had been a fair bit older than him and had died after a difficult struggle with breast cancer.

Much to my amazement, he even asked to come to church with me one day, although he found the modern worship band far too much and longed I think for a more traditional service structure.

So, I finally had a boyfriend – and one I knew my parents would adore.

The only trouble was that a few months after we started dating, Rebecca wrote to me to ask if she could come and stay as she was going to be travelling through London on her way back home to Europe.

I was lodging with an old school friend, Julia, who

happened to be my old head girl. In fact, I had played Bertrand de Poulengey to her St Joan in her final year. We had met out of the blue one Sunday when we both happened to sit on the back pew of a church on Parson's Green, St Dionis, run by Shaun and Anne Atkins. It was one of those coincidences that I was starting to find 'normal'. I was desperate to find a new flat for a bit while I tried to sell my house in Kent and buy something in London. Julia was desperate to have a lodger. I moved in that afternoon.

Fortunately, Julia didn't seem to mind me having a guest, as long as it was only for a few nights, but stressed she would need to stay in my room as she needed to keep the lounge free.

I thought it would be a good idea for Rebecca to meet Geoff – indeed, they were both keen to meet each other as they had by now heard quite a bit about each other.

I decided I would cook, and so we had what must be one of the most awkward dinner parties I've ever had to host. I say awkward, the truth is the two of them had a terrific time, teasing me mercilessly. The awkwardness was all with me, as I soon began to realise that my feelings for Rebecca were of a completely different magnitude to those I had for my dear Geoff.

Yes, I liked him – he was a kind, funny, caring, loving, intelligent man. The only problem was that I really didn't feel that physically attracted to him – well not in the way that my body seemed to be telling me it was to Rebecca.

As I write this, the older me looks back at the younger me with great sadness. I now realise I had no understanding at all of the nature of desire. How could I? How was I supposed to know what I 'should be feeling' when I had never felt it before? I realise now that's what I found so confusing. Here I was with a man who was perfectly eligible, in fact a 'very good match.' So, what was wrong with me? Why was I so fixated on someone who was so 'out of bounds'? Why couldn't I feel for him what I kept – against my wishes – longing for with her?

Later that evening as I lay in bed, with Rebecca on a made-up bed beside me on the floor, I thought my head and my heart were going to explode. Tears sprung up from nowhere and sensing something was up, Rebecca asked me if I was okay.

The truth was I yearned to know whether what I longed for with her would bring me happiness. I wanted to touch her – I wanted to kiss her, just once. Please, could I do just that? I've no idea whether she had come with any intention of exploring that with me, but I realise now that talking about it in that way definitely 'killed the moment'. She was resolute in her answer – no.

And so began a living hell.

I decided to throw caution to the wind and sought out the views on 'sex before marriage' from a close Christian couple who I respected, and who I knew had slept together before they themselves had got married. After a couple of long talks, I decided that there was a theological case for it being permissible if we were truly 'committed to each other'. I immediately rang Geoff and asked if I could come over as I wanted to spend the night with him. He was stunned but delighted.

My hope was that if our relationship turned fully sexual, then things might change in how I felt about him. But sadly, it seemed to make no difference at all. Yes, of course we could have a 'good time', but at the back of my mind was always how I had felt lying next to Rebecca.

I started to become ill with various unusual aches and pains, which my chiropractor was convinced were related to my gall-bladder. After one particularly bad episode I was taken straight into the Cromwell Hospital, where I underwent a series of tests. At the end of it all the consultant came to see me and said: 'Jayne, we really can't find anything wrong with you. There's no doubt that you are in significant pain, but if you ask me, your body is incredibly stressed. You need a break.'

In the Chair

I was indeed stressed.

Work was a nightmare. The consultancy firm, McKinsey, had been brought in a month or so earlier to help us reform the way we 'did' marketing in the BBC. I say 'us' – which in fact was a small working group of senior BBC personnel who like me also found the restructuring extremely stressful. Indeed, shortly after I entered the Priory I heard that one of my colleagues on the group had sadly died of a heart attack.

I hated my job and tried to resign – on numerous occasions. Each time Pam would smile at me and say: 'Just try to hang in there, Jayne, we'll all get through this very soon.' I took to printing off, signing and dating my resignation letter each morning – a rather unusual move now I come to think about it, but at least it gave me some sense of control over a situation that was totally out of control. Perhaps I should have heeded the warning signs, particularly since the phrase that kept continuously bouncing around my head was 'Stop the world, I want to get off!'

The sad thing was that I had so much to be proud of with what I had been able to achieve. As I was to learn later, after I had left, I had done some truly ground-breaking work in understanding the nature of the differing BBC television brands. The most fascinating had been the challenges of how BBC2 was perceived by the younger generation, who saw it as the 'old man's gardening channel'. But they watched it – thanks to the Friday Night Comedy Zone that we had created – far more than Channel 4. However, because they saw the latter as the 'hip and trendy' channel, they attributed the Comedy Zone programmes directly to it, rather than to the BBC. As a result, they refused to believe they were getting good value from the BBC licence fee.

I gave a full presentation of these findings and recommendations to the BBC Controller, Michael Jackson, just before I went into hospital – and just before he went off to head up Channel 4.

———•———

I tried to find solace and support at church. Sadly, however, St Paul's Onslow Square was itself going through a very difficult time as it had just been announced it was to close so that Nicky and Sila Lee could go back to Holy Trinity Brompton to set up their Marriage Course. Our assistant vicar, Stuart Lees, was going to move to be the vicar of Christ Church, Fulham and John Peters, our curate, was going to stay in the current building until he could find another church to move into.

We were each asked to decide who we wanted to follow. It was truly awful – a large but close-knit church family were forcibly 'split up' and asked to decide whose ministry they wanted to be part of. I chose to stay with John, along with a clear majority of the 20-30 something brigade.

It was around this time that a dynamic street preacher came over from New York and gave what must be one of the most important sermons I've ever heard in my life.

I've no idea who he was, although I do remember that he worked with kids and the homeless.

His faith was raw and real, so much so that he lived 'completely by faith' (as he called it), trusting God for every penny. The challenge he had for us was this – were we prepared to trust God enough to do the same? How real was *our* faith? If God was truly God, how far were we prepared to go to follow Him?

I was, as usual, sitting near the back. I'd long decided that this was by far the safest place to sit, far away from the charismatic antics that went on at the front afterwards, and of which I was still quite wary. To qualify, I wasn't at all wary of the Holy Spirit. It was just the people who professed to have received certain gifts and who, when prayed for, seemed to fall down all the time – even though I was sure some of them were being pushed.

Anyway, I remember sitting and listening to this guy and thinking that he had a point. If God was truly God, how was I going to let that affect my life?

I bowed my head, and decided my best strategy was to be as honest as possible before God:

'Dear Lord,

I know that you are God, that you love me and that you want the best for me.

I want to do whatever it is you want me to do with my life, as I know that will bless me the most, but please there's just three things I'd ask:

One – please don't take my car, it's my only real indulgence. (I did tend to have a thing for nice cars.)

Two – please don't take my job, I know I hate it, but it's my whole identity. (Being able to say I was Head of Marketing at the BBC seemed to hold a fair amount of sway back then.)

Three – please don't send me to India. (It was the one place I'd been that I had found so utterly overwhelming, where the scale of need was so much bigger than anything I had ever seen before.)

In Your Mighty Name, Amen'.

It was a totally honest prayer – I laid it all out, and I really meant every word of it.

The only thing is – one should never try bargaining with God. I can tell you now, it never works!

Within a week I'd had to sell my car in order to make the down-payment for my new flat; within a month I had been signed off ill from the BBC, and would never return, and my first consultancy job (after I had recovered from my breakdown) was for ... you guessed it ... Mission India!

No kidding.

———•———

So, back to sitting in the chair at the Priory. There I was sitting in this cold, stark room with my psychiatrist, trying not to get angry with her for suggesting I should just 'change my religion'.

I realise now, of course, that what she was trying to tell me was that I couldn't change my sexuality.

I wish she had said that – we could have at least had a useful conversation about that. But to just tell me to change my religion showed me that she had absolutely no idea how precious my faith was to me. It also put her very firmly in the 'secular' box, which meant I found her opinions regarding my faith hard to take seriously or trust.

She did, however, suggest that I should start a therapy programme at the Priory to help structure my days as I rebuilt my strength.

To be fair, no one had used the term 'breakdown' directly with me, but we all knew that was what had happened. I'd collapsed on the floor of the BBC carpark after having gone to see my GP. My normal GP was off ill and so I had been seen by a young 'fresh out of medical school' locum who had told me there was nothing wrong with me. Picking myself up off the floor, I had managed to crawl in to my office, lock the door and call Geoff. He came immediately and was met by a woman in floods of tears, who couldn't string a sentence together.

He took me home. I never went back.

My tests in the Cromwell Hospital had been just two weeks previously, and I had been virtually non-functional since then. In fact, I had hidden away in my four-television-screen office hoping no one would disturb me. (Seniority at the BBC was in those days measured in TV screens. Four was quite a lot; my boss had six, and my team just one.)

I had gone to bed and slept, a lot.

In the Chair

Luckily, I'd just moved into my new flat – which had been a stress of its own, even if it was my dream flat and a major answer to prayer. Knowing how happy I had been in Paris, I had prayed that I would somehow find a similar flat, with a mezzanine level and a large open space going up into the rafters. The very first flat I saw was just that – on Rockley Road, right next to St Simons.

The only problem was that I couldn't afford it, but thanks to another major 'coincidence' I was able to knock £10k off the asking price. As 'chance' would have it, I received a card on my return from Australia from a couple who I had met on holiday a few years before, inviting me to supper. He, John, just happened to be an architect, who just happened to have done the renovation to the flat next door to the one I was buying (what are the chances of that in the whole of London?), and therefore just happened to know a few things about my flat that would affect the asking price.

I have no doubt God *can* answer prayers, I've seen it happen far too often. My question is always, will He choose to *this* time?

———•———

The result of my discussions with my psychiatrist was that I agreed to attend the Priory as a day patient. I also decided to get a little kitten, Harry, for company. Sadly, I had felt it best to break up with Geoff – I was just in too much of a mess to have a relationship.

I had good days and bad days; well, mostly bad days. And they got worse. Sometimes I couldn't even decide what food to buy – I'd go to the supermarket and stare at the shelves and then come home empty handed, crying as I realised that even the basic decisions were just far too much.

I was appointed a counsellor called Gerry, and the moment I met him I realised I was going to have a problem. He was exactly my 'older man' type, which he knew. I talked to my psychiatrist about it, but she told me to trust the process – and him. That was the start of an even greater hell.

How could my doctor be also my illness and my drug?

It was impossible – and ultimately, I would be proved right in my concerns.

He suggested I became a patient of the Galsworthy Addiction clinic, which formed part of the Priory hospital, as he thought I was 'addicted to work'. By means of incentive he explained that this would result in me being able to see more of him. I said yes immediately.

There were some funny moments I suppose, like the time a young alcoholic medic, called Charlie, and I were sent out into the woods to do some 'scream therapy' together. We were told that this would help us get in touch with our inner anger – all we needed to do was to start screaming at each other. We walked off into Richmond Park, which bordered the Priory, and after a few minutes I turned to Charlie and suggested we gave it a go. Both of us felt highly embarrassed, so I agreed to go first. I laughingly looked at him and let out a roar. Charlie roared back at me, which seemed to release something in him – so he continued with gusto. He was starting to go rather red in the face, when a loud voice came over a megaphone: 'It's okay, ma'am, we're here now – you're safe!' I looked up and saw we were surrounded by blue flashing lights – it turns out we had got the local police quite worried.

There were of course some very tough days, many of which are too painful to recount here. We had various group exercises, all aimed at helping us connect with our pain. I remember being asked which part of my body I hated the most and answering, much to everyone's astonishment, 'my brain'. That said, I was surprised when the models always answered something like, 'my face' or 'my legs'.

There was one group exercise which stands out the most, primarily for the major levels of embarrassment I felt. It was also the day that things became much clearer for my counsellors.

We were told a story, which I now realise was an allegory for a sexual liaison between a couple. We were then asked to draw what we had heard. Now, I can't draw at the best of times, and so I just drew stick men and women doing whatever they had done in the story. Finally, we had to show our pictures to the rest of the group. They all laughed when they saw mine, which made me mortified. What had I got wrong? Gerry said my pictures looked very innocent and asked if I'd understood the real nature of the story. I said I obviously hadn't and he then asked me why I thought that might be – I paused, bit my lip, and finally replied, 'Because I've been raped, but I really don't want to go there, and I definitely don't want to talk about it.'

It did at least stop the group laughing and allowed me the space to acknowledge for the first time what happened back in Newcastle. I also realised I felt completely shut down about it all.

The one thing I found extremely helpful was the art therapy classes, which were led by a counsellor who I later learnt was also part of my church. The purpose of the class was to create something that depicted a key moment in the meditation that we had just been taken through.

The first week the meditation was about diving down into the sea to retrieve some treasure in a chest on the sea floor. The only thing I could think about was that amazing feeling of coming up into the open air when you've been down underwater for a while. Everything is 4-dimensional, and you can hear sounds like you've never heard them before. I created a collage that tried to replicate that 'breakthrough' moment and realised that that was what I too was longing for.

The next week was a completely different scenario. I was in a closed room with the door locked, but I could see that there was light outside. The door eventually opened, and I was let out. For me, what stood out was the fact that I could see light around the doorframe. Yes, I was in a dark box, but there was still a crack of light – that is hope – around the outline of the doorframe. Light will always shine through and conquer darkness, and I knew one day my door would also open.

I used to paint that crack of light for various friends in the Priory. It was a painting that I myself would keep – and it saw me through some of the toughest days of my life. It gave me hope.

———•———

But things got complicated – especially with Gerry, and I was eventually told I was being moved to another hospital. I went into shock. Who could I trust now? What had I done wrong? What in fact *was* wrong with me? The latter was a very key question, and one that the new hospital found impossible to answer. They thought I was perfectly fine, if not a bit heartbroken and depressed.

Luckily, 'out of the blue' a friend from church turned up to visit me who wanted to tell me about a person who had really helped her at a very low point in her life. She introduced me to Dr Robert Lefever, who ran a place called PROMIS down in Kent. Robert met me, heard my story, and suggested what I really needed was to be somewhere safe where I could take time to heal.

I completely agreed and admitted myself into his care.

Sadly, this started an even darker period of my life, but one that would eventually lead to a breakthrough – and the story at the very start of this book.

———•———

I realised that this was going to be a very different experience to the Priory when, on check in, I was told that I had to turn in my keys, my purse, my violin, my music, my books and any medication I had brought with me. On asking why, I was told that we were not allowed anything we could 'use' on (a phrase that is applied to addicts to stop them feeling pain – which can be anything from coffee, chocolate and cigarettes to substances such as alcohol, gambling and drugs).

Confused and a bit surprised I decided to 'go with it' and was shown to my room – a shared dorm with two other girls. I panicked – this really wasn't what I had bargained for and would mean that I would be even more hesitant about telling anyone about my inner struggles over my sexuality.

PROMIS practiced the 12 STEP programme for addicts. I asked what they thought my addiction was, and they said they were looking into it, but from my brief conversation with Robert probably 'work addiction' or 'love addiction'. The latter was news to me. Having never actually been in a situation of real love (unrequited love perhaps), I found it quite an uncomfortable label. It seemed even more inappropriate when I was sent to Sex Addicts Anonymous as part of my therapy. Goodness, I'd hardly ever had sex – but I did find the other people's stories heart breaking.

In fact, I found the whole experience of PROMIS heart breaking. I see it as one of the greatest privileges of my life to have spent four months with people who were literally fighting for their lives and carrying some of the most horrific burdens that no human being should have to carry.

It has challenged me to my core as to how I relate to those suffering from alcohol and drug addiction – and how society treats them. I salute their courage to keep going, against all the odds.

I think of an Angolan broadcaster, brought to the centre by his embassy, suffering obviously from a very serious drink problem. He refused to talk for the first few weeks, but when he and I were watching a documentary commemorating Princess Diana's visit to Angola to clear landmines, he started to sing a child's song. Given I spoke French, we started to talk. A few days later he asked if I would be a witness to his story.

The war had broken him. It had taken his whole family – he had come home one day and found body parts of his children and wife strewn all over his garden.

I think of Sarah, just out of her teens, whose parents had both been social workers. When her mother left her father, he assumed that she would – at the age of 14 – take her place in every way. In the kitchen, in his bed, as mother to her two younger brothers. She had tried to tell another social worker, but they hadn't believed her. She turned to alcohol and then tried to take her life.

It was Sarah who wrote me a little poem, the first line of which simply said:

'Failure is never falling down – It's staying down!'

There are so many stories, that bring with them so many tears. What was worse that we were all it seems, including myself, totally cut off from our pain, utterly unable to connect with it.

I remember this vividly when one day a young Geordie heroin addict arrived and described a 'typical day' in her life. I sat and wept quietly as I heard how her life was made up of stealing from her friends and family and prostituting herself just to get a fix. She looked at me and asked me blankly why I was crying – 'Because it's so sad,' I mumbled, 'you're so young, and it's just so very sad'. What was worse was that she really thought her life was 'normal'.

Then one day a woman arrived, well known to many across Britain, who was going to become a close friend of mine but also wreak complete havoc in my head. We'll call her Joanne.

She was uncontrollable – drink and hard drugs had made her wild, and so physically strong that no one could hold her down. She ran away one night – predictably to the pub – and was brought back to the house. At around one o'clock in the morning I was woken by the nurse, who asked me if I could go and help. I went down to the special 'detox unit' and saw that the side window was smashed. Joanne was sat with blood pouring from her arm – she'd put her fist through the window trying to break out.

'She won't let anyone get near her and keeps asking for you,' the nurse explained.

I went in and sat with her and listened. Her pain raw, her anger red. She let me pull some of the glass out of her arm, and then finally let the nurse dress it. I said I'd stay with her a bit.

Joanne went off to the bathroom and then, much to my amazement, came back completely naked. It was the first time I had ever seen another woman stand in front of me like that, that. So utterly beautiful – which arguably was why she was a model. My own feelings went into overdrive. I gulped, and suggested it was time she went to bed.

She let me pull back the sheets of her single bed, and got dutifully in. I pulled the sheets up and sat down on the bed side and smoothed her hair – this poor woman just needed some love and someone she could trust, I thought. We had a strong bond, but neither of us had ever talked about it. I reached down to give her a kiss on the cheek, but she moved her head and caught me, full on the lips. It took me completely off guard, but I responded immediately, and a new world came into life.

My first real kiss.

———————•·•———————

It was enough to send me into a spiral though, which when combined with other events at PROMIS, all became nearly too much to bear.

Sadly, I've always had quite a few gynaecological problems which have led to very painful periods. When I am stressed these tend to get worse. In addition, after years of medication I have found that only a few types of painkillers work effectively without causing me other types of side effects.

Robert didn't believe in medicating period pain, or so it seemed. Nor did he believe in antidepressants. All my medication was taken off me when I arrived, and I was informed that I would have to go 'cold turkey'. Luckily, I found a way of coping with the effects of coming rapidly off the anti-depressants, but the lack of period pain medication caused me significant distress.

After one particularly vile day, where I was doubled up in pain and trying not to throw up in the process, I decided I needed to go somewhere that was safe. I had come to the conclusion that PROMIS was not that safe a place, but was in fact another form of living hell.

My only option, I felt, was to run away.

I had no money, no phone, no car, nothing.

The only place I could think of going was the local church which we sometimes walked passed on a Sunday when, if we were lucky, we were allowed out – always supervised and always in twos.

We were right in the heart of the Kent countryside, and I had no map.

I must have walked for hours – in the rain – before I finally came across the church. It was a typical quaint little parish church, as ancient as the village it was part of. I went up to the old wooden door and tried to open it. It was locked.

I was distraught. Even God had closed His doors to me.

I stumbled down the path and back into the village. The rain was getting heavier and I was exhausted. There was a pub in the village, so I decided to go in and take refuge there for a bit.

To this day I wish I could remember the name of the village, and the pub – and the landlord, who kindly looked at me and realised all was not well. 'Are you okay, love?' he gently said, seeing how drenched and upset I was.

No, I explained, I was not. Did he know the vicar of the church, please? Did they live nearby?

He went off behind the bar and came back with a phone number. There was a phone box down the road, he told me. I think he must have given me 10p or I must have reversed the charges.

This wonderful female vicar – the first I'd ever met – came and opened the church for me. She sat down in the choir stalls with me and reassured me she was there to just listen. I started to heave with tears, the pain coming in waves. I tried to speak, but words wouldn't form. So, we sat, and she held my hand, and we prayed.

Eventually I was able to try and explain a little of what had happened. I think she had probably guessed I was from PROMIS. What else would I be doing out there in the middle of nowhere?

She listened and then asked me what I wanted to do? I just said I wanted to go home. I'd had enough, and I just wanted to go back home to my flat in London.

She put me in her car and drove me back to PROMIS so I could get my things.

(Please, you wonderful woman of God, if you're out there reading this – please do contact me.)

The next day I left, went back to London, and went to bed – hoping never to wake up again.

'Ah Jayne, but you can respond in love to any situation I put you in, because I AM love.

I AM in you, and you are in Me!'

Almost a year to the day later I was sat in the Archbishop of Canterbury's study in Lambeth Palace, along with the Archbishop of York and the Secretary General, Philip Mawer, being interviewed as one of the six Appointed Members of the newly formed Archbishops' Council.

Afterwards I would walk across the bridge to the Houses of Parliament, where I would have lunch with someone who would become a dear friend during my time on the Council.

A few days later I would then get in my car and drive to Highgrove (Prince Charles's private home) for an interview with the trustees of the Prince's Trust.

God has a way of redeeming things – but never the way we expect.

CHAPTER SIX

From Prince to Pauper

Autumn 1997

The journey of how I was appointed to the Archbishops' Council, is an extraordinary story – which by now I hope you're sort of expecting.

Following my bedroom encounter with Mr God, I lay back in my bed and wondered what I should do next. To be honest, I sensed immediately what it was going to be, but I couldn't believe I was being asked to do it.

'Go back?! You mean you want me to go back to PROMIS?. To that place that has caused me such great pain and where I felt so abused?!'

Yes, I was to go back, to submit myself to the process and stay there till I was clear it was the right time to leave. I've no idea why I was having to undergo this, but I *knew* it was the right thing to do – even if it was the last thing I personally *wanted* to do.

So, I entered a version of my own passion – allowing the world to throw at me what it could. The only difference was that this time I was a different person as I was going with the knowledge that God was with me. Indeed, I knew that somehow my God of Love would help me face anything.

———•———

It was extremely hard. I was put in a room with a self-styled 'white witch', who was convinced I was the devil. Joanna had gone, and then come back, and was all over the place in relation to me.

There was plenty else besides, but that is not for the recounting here.

Eventually, one Sunday, after a particularly gruelling group therapy session where I was Robert's 'chosen subject', I finally decided it was time to leave. I had run the course and, I believed, passed my test. I had the sense that Robert and the other counsellors agreed that too.

I went home to London. Unsure what to do next I decided to go and visit my parents in Guernsey.

It was while I was there that my vicar's wife, Jenny, called, and asked if she could have a chat. She had heard that I had been unwell and wanted to know how things were going. We talked pleasantly for a bit, but I didn't really feel like sharing too much – I didn't know her well enough.

After a few minutes she paused and said: 'Jayne, do you mind me saying something … it's just, you do sound incredibly angry with God.'

'Angry with God? How could I be?' I thought. 'Have you any idea what I've just been through?'

I said thank you and closed the conversation down. I was put out, upset and I didn't know how best to process any of it. So, I decided to go for a walk on the cliffs – just a few fields over the road from our home. The more I thought about it as I walked though, the more I realised she was right.

I *was* indeed angry with God, very angry.

Yes, I might have had a revelation about His unconditional love, but why on earth had He allowed me to go through so much? Why had He caused me such confusion with Louise, Tatjana, Rebecca and Joanna? Hadn't I given my life to trying to do the right thing, and now look where I was at? And why had I had to go through everything at the Priory and PROMIS?

From Prince to Pauper

All I wanted, all I ever wanted, was to be loved! Why, oh why, was that coming from the one source that was 'forbidden fruit'? I was caught in a catch-22. How could all this be the will of a 'loving' God?

I came home, picked up the phone, and rang Jenny back. She answered immediately. I thanked her and told her she was absolutely right – I *was* angry with God.

'That's okay, Jayne, that's okay. The thing is – have you told Him? He's big enough, He can take it!'

This last two phrases blew my mind. Had I told Him? How could I tell Him – He was God. He knew anyway, didn't He? And how could I be angry with Him? He was God, who always knew best!

But somehow the essence of what she said resonated deeply – if my relationship with God was going to mean anything, then it had to be *real*, and I therefore had to be real with Him. Real about what I was truly feeling. No more 'should and ought' about what I 'should' be feeling. No more pretending to feel things that I thought I 'ought' to be feeling when I wasn't. I just needed to connect with the reality of my raw emotions and be one hundred per cent honest about where I was at. Then I realised God could meet me in that space, and we could walk forward together.

It was a truly *kairos* moment for me – a revelation that would change my life for ever.

Thank you, Jenny.

———•———

Later, when I was on the Archbishops' Council, I would reflect that it was this that I believed God wanted us to do as a Church. Get down on our knees and be honest – really honest – about where we were at and the problems we were facing. We then needed to be honest that we no longer had any of the answers, that we didn't know what to do, that we could no longer cope, and that we desperately needed His help.

Then, and only then, could He come and intervene.

It's what I believed then – and it's what I still believe He wants us to do now.

I tried to get back into a semi-normal routine, but I felt broken on the inside and hadn't a clue how to put the various bits of myself back together.

My issues around sexuality were just part of a large complex jigsaw, which at the time I put down to a level of emotional brokenness that stemmed from various events that had happened to me in my past.

I decided I needed emotional healing and went to talk to the one person at my church who I thought could help. She was a highly respected counsellor, and she in turn kindly put me in touch with a wonderful woman – Sue Stanley – who ran a small Christian charity called The Susannah Trust.

This little organisation was based in Harley Street, and worked to form a bridge between the Church and the mental health profession. Sue agreed to see me, and after an initial assessment, suggested that I see her colleague – Dr Gaius Davies, an eminent Christian psychiatrist – who could assess me and give me his opinion as to what was troubling me and what I should do.

I had a couple of sessions with him, which I found extremely helpful – just being listened to, with no 'tough love' or group therapy to have to endure or fear, that enabled me to unpack certain things, interspersed with his wise insightful questions.

After the second session, Gaius looked at me and said, 'Jayne, I really don't think you're an addict. I'm not sure why they've put you through all that they have, but quite frankly I think you've been treated appallingly. For my part you are heart broken, depressed and conflicted.'

From Prince to Pauper

I could have hugged him. I've only once had to wait for test results to say whether or not I had cancer and receiving the 'all clear' from my consultant was much like how I now felt then.

I thanked Gaius and Sue and asked if there was anything I could do to help them in return – especially as they had each seen me on a pro-bono basis. A couple of days later, Sue rang and asked if I'd consider becoming one of their trustees.

I was taken completely off guard. Me, a trustee? I'd never been asked to be a trustee before.

It was my first step into the Charity Sector, and one from which I would not look back.

———•———

The issue of money, or rather the lack of it, is something worth touching on here as these years were the start of a journey into trusting God in ways that many around me would find challenging.

I had for some of my time in hospital been paid by the BBC, who then sought to 'do a deal' to get me off their books. Luckily, I had some medical insurance, but this ran out towards the end of my time at the Priory.

Out of the blue, in a pattern that I would start to find all too familiar, I received a request from a friend of a friend who lived in Italy. She and her husband were wondering if they could possibly rent my flat for the dates I just happened to be in the Priory. Then, just as they left, I received another request from an old friend – Jonathan from Newcastle days– asking if he too could rent my flat around the time I was in PROMIS. So, at least I had a way of covering the mortgage.

With no job and no therapy, I now had significant time on my hands. Having received a final payment from the BBC, I decided a holiday was in order and took myself off to visit my cousins in Hong Kong. From there I went on to China and Thailand, where I met all sorts of fascinating people, many of whom just happened to be connected in some way with my past.

I came home and began to worry about what I would do next. I then unexpectedly received a call from Oxford Corporate Consultants (OCC), a consultancy firm staffed with mostly ex-Procter & Gamble colleagues, several of whom I had worked for previously. They offered me a part-time post, that would pay me more than I had been on whilst full time at the BBC. It seemed a no-brainer, but I was concerned I wasn't yet strong enough to go back to that kind of cut-throat business world.

I asked for time to think about and went off down to Plymouth to do a Day Skipper sailing course – the one thing I had promised myself that I would do if I ever survived the Priory and PROMIS.

It was when I was on the train down to Plymouth that I happened to see an advert in the *Sunday Times*, featuring two clergymen on a bridge. It was inviting people to apply for something called 'the Archbishops' Council'. It explained they were looking for six people to work as voluntary non-executive directors. I remember reading the it and thinking: 'Gosh, that's the last thing I would want to do.'

I got off the train, walked down to the boat and put the newspaper in the bin.

Everything possible then started to go wrong on the boat. The engine refused to start, one of the sheets got stuck, the mast needed mending. I began to feel like Jonah, and knew that I had to go back, get the paper out of the bin, and phone the number to request an application pack.

It's just as well I did as when I returned home a week later, I realised that the closing date for applications was the very next day. Apprehensively, but with a sense that something was happening beyond my control, I filled out the form and drove it round to Church House.

I asked Sue Stanley if she would be one of my referees, and

she excitedly said she would be delighted. More importantly she urged me to meet a good friend of hers – Viscountess Gill Brentford, who was a close friend of the then Archbishop of Canterbury, the Most Revd George Carey.

Gill met me for coffee a week or so later, and asked me which diocese I was in. 'Diocese?' I said, rather confused, 'What's a diocese?' She laughed and said jokingly: 'Next you'll be telling me you don't know how many Archbishops we have?' 'One?' I innocently offered.

I mean, how was I supposed to know?

I worshipped in a church which although nominally Anglican didn't really have anything to do with the formal structures of the Church of England. Like so many others of its kind, it just happened to meet in one of its buildings. We were all Christians, surely that was what counted most?

Gill suggested that it would probably be helpful for me to learn a little about the Church of England. I wholeheartedly agreed but needed her advice as to how I might go about doing so. She recommended a little booklet and mentioned that I might also want to try to attend the York General Synod. Seeing the blank look on my face, she went on to explain what General Synod was. It all seemed a complete anathema to me, and I wondered why on earth I was being drawn into this completely foreign world – but something inside me kept willing me on.

———•———

Remembering I had promised to call Gina back from OCC but unsure of what to say to her, I sat and prayed. I told God that I was going to turn the job down, as I felt it was just too much for me. I did add that if that was the wrong decision, could He please make it blatantly clear to me?

I waited, nothing happened. So, I rang Gina.

'Oh Jayne, we're so glad you've called – we've been

wondering how you are? Before you say anything more, I think there's something I need to be up front with you about and tell you. You may not know this, but we are in fact a Christian partnership – though we don't tend to tell folk that – and we all really believe that you are meant to come and work with us. So how about it?'

How could I refuse? It seemed 'on a plate' in the circumstances.

It did at least mean that I was back in a seriously impressive job as I was going through my application for the Archbishops' Council.

I did go to the York Synod, and sat up in the balcony wondering what on earth I was doing there. There were a few people who really stood out to me from the interventions that they made, and on passing them in the corridor I happened to say as much to them – Father David Holding and Dr Christina Baxter to name but two. How was I to know that they would eventually end up being colleagues of mine on the Archbishops' Council, and with whom I would work so closely?

Back in London, Sue rang me to say she had just unexpectedly received an invite to a fundraising event at Lambeth Palace the next week in aid of St George's Crypt, Sheffield. She wondered if I would like to go with her as her guest? It seemed too big a coincidence to say no – even more so when I later found out that it was the night before the archbishops had to decide who they wanted to interview. As it so happened, the one person Sue knew at the event was a certain Colin Fletcher, who just happened to be the Archbishop of Canterbury's chaplain. Colin and I were duly introduced, and he then decided to introduce me to George himself. It meant that the Archbishop and I were able to have a chat so that I could explain my interest in standing for the Council.

I began to sense that somehow this was 'all meant to be', and that independent of whatever I did, God had a plan. I submitted myself to it – mindful of the prayer I had prayed the previous year.

———•———

The trouble was that I felt horrendously ill-equipped to deal with anything to do with the Church, especially anything theological. I decided the best thing to do was to write to the one person I respected the most, and who many saw as the 'Father' of evangelicals – the Revd Dr John Stott.

A few weeks later I found myself in his study at Langham Place, having been invited to tea.

Sitting there I suddenly realised that I didn't really know what to actually ask him. It had seemed like a good idea to approach him as I felt that I needed a crash course in evangelical doctrine, but I didn't quite know how to say that and recognised it sounded quite a presumptuous request.

We talked about all the 'coincidences' that had happened to date, and how I felt that there was a good chance that I might get appointed to this new Council. Much to my surprise he then offered me an opportunity that I had no idea even existed, and yet was exactly what I needed. Unknown to me, Dr Stott ran a summer school each year for evangelical clergy from around the world to help train them in theology. He wondered whether I would also like to attend as his guest?

I couldn't believe it – a training course! What's more, it happened to start just as I was coming to an end of a major project with OCC. It was extraordinary, and such a blessing to be with so many inspirational clergy from around the world. I felt I was on my very own mini-Lambeth conference.

The course covered almost everything I could have dreamed of, and I will be forever grateful to Uncle John (as he was affectionately known) for his kindness and generosity in letting me attend.

Interestingly, we did have one minor disagreement during

the final questions that followed his Valedictory Sermon. He had been urging us to go out and do whatever we felt able to do for the sake of the Gospel. I rather strongly disagreed with this and said that there were far too many people 'out there' doing things they thought needed to be done, but what we really needed to do was to learn to listen and do only that which we were actively directed by God to do. Uncle John disagreed, saying that that would only lead to inaction – I disagreed again, to the surprise of my classmates, saying we needed instead to get better at hearing the inner voice of God.

Fortunately, he agreed with me on that.

Funnily enough, the next time I saw him was in 2005 in the West Wing of the White House! He and Baroness Cox had just addressed a meeting of the White House Staff's Christian Fellowship, and I had somehow been able to gate-crash the lunch with them in the President's private restaurant afterwards. Once another chair had been added to the table, we were given menus with the best of American fayre – chicken in a basket, hamburgers or Caesar salads!

———•———

The night before my interview with the Archbishops I was asked by a friend to join him at a prayer meeting at the Emmanuel Centre on Marsham Street. To be honest I felt a bit 'prayed out' by this stage, so instead I said I would meet him for a drink afterwards. It was raining and at 10pm there was no sign of him. I crept into the back of the auditorium and realised that the meeting was still in full swing. A visiting Argentinian pastor called Ed Silvoso was finishing giving his 'word', which was about people being at major crossroads in their lives. He wanted to pray for anyone who felt that might be them and invited us all to come out to the front for ministry.

I remember smiling to myself and thinking 'Here we go, Mr God', and making my way – with dozens of others – to the front. The ministry team stepped forward and I realised that few were actually going to get prayed for by Mr Silvoso himself.

I stood and waited my turn and was a little surprised when I looked up and saw Ed Silvoso standing right in front of me. 'What's your name?' he asked in his thick Spanish accent. I told him, and said I had an important meeting the next day with senior members of the Church of England. We bent our heads to pray. After a few minutes of praying in tongues, he looked up at me rather strangely and said: 'Jayne, I have a very unusual word for you – you are going to be the "Archbishop's helpmate". Does that mean anything to you?' I think my face said it all as I explained exactly who I was being interviewed by. He just smiled, and we committed the whole process to the Lord.

Everything seemed to be in hand.

The one thing that didn't seem to be going so well, however, was my consultancy job with OCC.

I had had a couple of fascinating marketing projects, which I had enjoyed considerably, but as we approached the summer I had been put on a project to work with a client which eventually led to me being asked to help launch a new range of alcopops. I felt incredibly uneasy about this and said as much to my boss – I didn't want to be encouraging teenagers to drink.

I went home and prayed, confused as to why I had been put in such a difficult position.

Within a couple of hours my phone was ringing. It was an old head hunter friend who had rung to see if I was at all interested in working with Prince Charles. I laughed out loud – remembering the letter I had sent all those years previously when I was at Cambridge – and said actually, yes, I had always had a thing about wanting to work for HRH. He explained they were looking for a new Director of Sales and Marketing for the Prince's Trust, and that given my background they were keen to meet me.

For some reason I seemed to by-pass a lot of the recruitment process and found myself fast-tracked and sitting in an armchair in Mark, the Chief Executive's, office. After a few minutes of standard questioning, Mark looked at me and threw his pile of briefing papers down onto the floor.

'There's something different about you, Jayne, and I want to know what it is!'

I swallowed hard and thought 'Not now, Lord, surely?', but then decided that given I was in a fairly unique situation anyway there was nothing to lose. Summoning all my courage I said: 'Well the thing is, Mark, I have a pretty strong faith – maybe that's what you can sense?'

The ensuing silence was deafening. I can still feel his eyes boring into me as I began to wonder how I could make a quick exit. After what felt like an age, but was probably only a minute, he said:

'Does that mean you can tell me what this Alpha course is all about, then? My wife's been on at me for ages to go, but I'm really not sure it's my thing.'

It must be one of the most unusual interviews I've ever had. We stayed talking for quite a while. He was adamant I should meet his trustees, and I took it as a highly likely 'done-deal' (given the number of coincidences I'd had to date) that this new job was very likely going to happen.

In an act that many thought ill-advised, but I believed to be the only honest way forward, I decided to tell OCC about my forthcoming interviews with the Prince's Trust. I also reiterated my serious concerns about working on the alcopop business. OCC said they understood, but that sadly there wasn't any other projects for me to work on at that time. We agreed therefore that I would step back, do the interview and that if it didn't work out I would come back to talk to them.

From Prince to Pauper

A day or so after my interview for the Archbishops' Council I found myself being shown into the ballroom at Highgrove. It felt like a scene out of *The Sound of Music*. I had been informed that tragically there had been a fatal boating accident the day before on a Prince's Trust holiday, and that they were having an emergency safeguarding meeting, which might take some time.

So, I sat in this impressive state room and went over my notes. Then went over them again. After about 20 minutes I started to get bored and decided to say as much to Mr God. 'What on earth am I doing here?' I remember thinking, to which one single very loud word came back: 'Pray!'

I stood up and started to walk around the room. It was one of those ballrooms with long glass windows that reached from floor to ceiling, in front of which were various wooden showcases displaying gifts from the Prince's travels from around the world. I decided to use these as 'prayer pointers', and walked round to each glass cabinet, praying for the countries that were represented. I had just finished circum-navigating the room when I was called in for my interview.

It was only later that Mark explained that there was about to be a state ball – in that very ballroom – in the next few days to celebrate the Prince's fiftieth birthday, and that representatives from nearly every country in the world would be present.

Make of that what you will, but I believe the Lord can put us in the most unusual of places for reasons that we never fully understand – the important thing is for us to be open and willing to do whatever He asks of us when we are there.

The interview went well, or so I thought. Mark seemed pleased, and said he would ring me later that evening, which he did.

'Jayne, I've good news and bad news…the good news is that they loved you. The bad news is that we had a meeting with His Royal Highness afterwards and he wants us to amalgamate all his charities into one. That means, I'm afraid, we're going to have to put a complete freeze on recruitment for the time being, until we've got things sorted. I'm so sorry, but we'll be in touch.'

I put the phone down and remember distinctly thinking: 'This is a fine mess you've got me into, Mr God. I've just got on the Archbishops' Council, but now I have no paid job to support it!'

'Trust me!' came the response, 'I've got you exactly where you're meant to be.'

So that's how I came to be on the Archbishops' Council just days before my thirtieth birthday, with a sense that I was meant to be 'living by faith' and trusting that somehow, if I was doing what Mr God wanted me to be doing, then He would make a way for it all to be possible.

It was going to mean an extraordinarily different lifestyle to the one I was used to – where I would never know from one week to the next how I was going to make ends meet.

But somehow, I did.

Just.

CHAPTER SEVEN

Preach it, Sister!

December 1998

'Boy, this is going to be different!' Archdeacon Pete Broadbent had, in one loud stage whisper, said what everyone else around the table was thinking.

We were sat in the largest meeting room at Church House – dozens of us squeezed around one large table, or so it felt.

The meeting had been called, it seemed, because I had innocently asked if the newly-appointed members could have an induction to the Church of England, as I assumed that the other five appointed members would, like myself, be completely new to it all. I was beginning to realise that only I and David Lammy, the two 'younger' members of Council, were the actual newbies.

No one, it turned out, wanted to miss this first pre-meeting. Even the Archbishops had come – as well as all the Chairs of all the Boards and Councils and all the senior Archbishops' Council staff.

We'd gone around the table introducing ourselves, and when it finally came around to me I had said:

'Well, I'm Jayne. I'm afraid I'm never going to remember all your titles and names, so couldn't we just call each other by our first names. After all, if we're not going to treat each other like equals then what's the point of us being here?'

It was the first of many seemingly innocent questions I was going to ask – such as 'What had the Council been set up by Synod to do?' I don't think I ever really received a clear answer to that ....

The Archbishops' Council had been years in the making. It was born out of Bishop Michael Turnbull's Report, *Working as One Body*, which had investigated why the Church Commissioners had got themselves into so much trouble in the early 1990s and 'lost' a very large sum of money. One of the problems, it seemed, was that there was no central strategy group that could bring everyone round one large table. In addition, there was no 'executive' for the Archbishops to 'make things happen'. The concept of an Archbishops' Council was therefore borne, modelled on a Bishop's Council, that would bring together all the senior members of the Church in one place.

The problem was that it seemed to have significant power, which was viewed by many as a threat – particularly by the House of Bishops.

The most contentious issue was the number of appointed members that the Archbishops were themselves allowed to appoint. These places had been created to ensure that there were the required skills sets around the table. It was also hoped that it would enable certain voices to be incorporated that wouldn't naturally be heard otherwise. Eventually it was agreed that 6 of the 19 places would fall into this category. The others were there either by merit of their roles (Archbishops, Prolocutors, Chair and Vice Chair of House of Laity and the First Estates Commissioner) or because they had been voted on to represent their colleagues on Synod (two bishops, two clergy and two lay members).

I was under no illusions – I knew that I ticked the 'strategic consultant' and 'marketing and communications' skill boxes, but I was *really* there because I was female, evangelical and 'young'.

Preach it, Sister!

The first official meeting of the Archbishops' Council was held in Lambeth Palace on 15 January 1999. We started with a Eucharist in Lambeth Chapel, and I was asked to do one of the readings. It was a strange reading, from Revelation 7, but as I read it I began to choke up remembering my friends back in PROMIS and the Priory – that all seemed so very far away now:

> 'They shall hunger no more, neither thirst anymore; neither shall the sun light on them, nor any heat. For the Lamb which is in the midst of the throne shall feed them, and shall lead them unto living fountains of waters: and God shall wipe away all tears from their eyes.'

The question of what we had been formed to do was still pressing on my mind, and I had found that the induction day had not made it as clear as I thought it would. So, I asked again.

'Ah yes', Philip Mawer, the Secretary General to the Archbishops' Council, replied, 'I think the bishops have been working on a paper about this.' I asked whether it was something that we too might all be able to reflect on and discuss at our next meeting, as I thought it was quite a key question.

A paper duly arrived in the post, and I took it upstairs to my office to read.

It was a densely typed document, which I realised was more of a theological exposition on the role of the House of Bishops and how this differed to the role of the Archbishops' Council.

I didn't understand it at all and told Mr God that in no uncertain terms. If I'm honest, I can still remember the laughter ringing round my head with the immediate reply: 'Neither do I, Jayne!'

I decided that the best thing to do was to draft a simple Vision, Mission and Objectives presentation, incorporating some shared values, so as to illustrate to the Archbishops and the Secretary General the sort of document that I thought was needed. I naturally didn't feel able to make this up myself, so I took my inspiration from Archbishop George's past presidential addresses to Synod.

Much to my horror, on receiving the agenda for the next meeting, I realised that my draft presentation had been tabled alongside that of the House of Bishops'. Not the best way of making friends and influencing people, I felt, especially with the bishops on Council.

Archbishop David Hope was in the chair, and after a short prayer, he introduced the two papers – remarking how completely different they were and asking Council members what they thought.

Perched nervously on the edge of my seat, I looked down at my pad and waited for what I assumed would be a kind but firm rebuttal from one of the more senior Council members.

Much to my amazement Dr Christina Baxter, Chair of the House of Laity, was the first to speak: 'This is terrific! It's exactly the sort of different approach we've been hoping for, and I think it's great!' Others started to concur, and I realised that something rather special was happening.

Relieved, I pushed back on my seat, and promptly slipped off and fell down onto the floor.

I was *so* embarrassed, although luckily hardly anyone seemed to notice. The one thing that did happen though was that as I climbed back onto my chair a very clear internal voice, which I have always associated with Mr God, said: 'Ask George if he wants French lessons.'

'What? Are you mad?' I thought. 'I can't possibly do that – do you realise how that will seem?!'

I don't think I've ever struggled with such an outrageous idea in my life. I wrestled with it during the whole meeting. In the end I decided I must have read somewhere that George was keen to learn French, but I knew to go and offer him lessons out of the blue would be seen as very strange.

I decided this was definitely time for another fleece. So, I prayed that if Archbishop George was on his own at the end of the meeting, then I would talk to him. I knew I was on safe ground with this as his schedule was always tightly packed and he never just 'stood around' after meetings.

But there he was, at the end of the meeting, standing on his own – and looking across at me.

The phrase 'Fool for Christ' just doesn't cut it sometimes.

So, I went up to him, tapped him lightly on the arm and said: 'I'm sorry, I don't really know what to call you, so I'm going to call you George.' He smiled and nodded. 'Err, I don't really know how to put this', I continued nervously, 'but I have this sense that you'd like to learn French, and I was wondering whether, if you did, then perhaps I could maybe try and help, as I used to live in Paris?'

George stepped back and stared at me. I began to wish the ground could swallow me up.

'My goodness, how do you know that?' he said slightly bemused. 'Yes, I am trying to learn. Can you come tomorrow morning perhaps and we'll have a go?'

I got home to hear my phone ringing. It was Veronica, a wise new friend who I had met through our church, and who just happened to be Archbishop George's Private Secretary.

'Jayne, I don't know how you managed it, but George has cleared his diary for tomorrow morning and said something about you giving him a French lesson. Is this really true?'

Veronica was an absolute God-send to me and became a key support during what was quite a lonely and challenging time. We soon became prayer partners – which was a major blessing as she was the only one I could talk about certain confidential matters with, given she was party to them already.

It was lonely. I was lonely.

The evangelical church from which I hailed had no interest

in Church of England politics, and in truth were more than a little scathing about me getting on to the Council. 'Jayne, let the dead bury the dead' was the initial response I got from my vicar, which wasn't exactly a promising start.

Later, on finding out that I should in fact now sit on my church's PCC, I asked to have tea with Sandy Millar to explain – somewhat to his surprise – that I was now evidently a member of Holy Trinity Brompton's PCC. This was because my own church, which was the remnant that had remained in St Paul's Onslow Square with John Peters, and which was trying to find a new building, was in his parish. Sadly, there was now quite a rift between the two churches, so it seemed quite fitting that I now found myself in a rather unusual bridge position between the two.

At Sandy's suggestion, Nicky Gumbel and Tricia Neil met with me for lunch every couple of months so that we could 'touch base' and see how we could best work together. I personally found these meetings a great encouragement and will always remain grateful to them for their support. However, it was all done on a relatively formal basis, where we talked about our differences over Church of England policy. I could never have told them about the French lessons, for instance.

Recognising I would need to find my own form of spiritual support, I reached out to some close friends from my church who responded by forming a Prayer Net around me. They were wonderful, and in the initial months we met to pray before every Council meeting. As my contact base expanded, so too did the Prayer Net. Eventually I formed an online group who I emailed regularly with updates and ongoing prayer requests – which often focused on my funding needs.

Spiritually I therefore began to feel quite supported, but emotionally I did still feel quite alone.

I was by now actively 'seeking my emotional healing' to address my unwanted attractions. At the same time, I felt that I was being called to give the years I was on Council 'to God'. This meant that

Preach it, Sister!

I did not believe I was supposed to be in a relationship during my time on Council, although I expected there to be someone (a man) waiting for me the moment I came off.

But if the days were lonely, the nights were even more so. I yearned for love. My longing formed a gaping hole that would swallow me up at times. Try as I might, no amount of prayer would fill it.

* * *

Archbishop George and I did speak a bit of French together, although to be fair we spent more time talking about the state of the Church. He asked if I could meet someone on his behalf – the head of a well-known PR Agency, who was keen to offer his advice and help to the Church.

It would be true to say that back then our relations with the media were poor; in fact they were worse than that – they were abysmal. To my mind, we had pulled up the drawbridge and retreated into our bunker. I remember being surprised when I first arrived on Council at all the amazing work that was going on within the Board of Social Responsibility. Concerned that I had never heard about any of it, I asked what their media strategy was. 'Media strategy?' said the Director of the Board, 'Oh no, we don't speak to the media. We've learnt the hard way, it's just not worth it.'

I'm glad to say things changed significantly during my time on Council, thanks in part to a group of us who were determined to see this important area prioritised with increased resources. Today we have a very proactive and professional group of PR and Media experts within both Church House and Lambeth Palace, which the national institutions make full use of.

Anyhow, I arranged to meet the PR director for lunch. On the day in question, I remember sitting in my car in a side-street in Mayfair wondering what on earth I was going to say and feeling totally out of my depth. How was I going to be able to pull this meeting off? I rang a friend and asked if we could pray. We did. She said she had two verses for me, which I have clung to ever since:

> 'But God chose the foolish things of the world to shame the wise; God chose the weak things of the world to shame the strong. God chose the lowly things of this world and the despised things—and the things that are not—to nullify the things that are.' (1 Corinthians 1: 27-28)

From that point on, whenever I felt completely inadequate on Council – which I frequently did – I would remember these verses and draw great strength from them.

I still do.

———— •• ————

Perhaps the most meaningful thing that came out of my time with Archbishop George was the plan to ensure a Christian moment of reflection during the Millennium celebrations at the Dome. But before we go there, we have my first year of Council to get through. It was a year in which I would also preach my first sermon, which would go down in our church's history as 'one of those nights'.

———— •• ————

Our third meeting of Archbishops' Council was far fierier than the first two. It was our first residential together, which was challenging in itself – as it involved me trying to run down the corridor in my dressing gown to get to the showers without bumping into a bishop en route.

During our previous meeting it had been suggested that it would be helpful for the Archbishops to set out their own visions of the Church. This they then did, each in turn – which most Council members were delighted to hear. Well, all but me. Much to my embarrassment I started to cry as they spoke – a fact I tried to hide by plugging the corner of my eyes with my fingers and burying my face in my hair. The Archbishops invited Council members to feed back their thoughts, and several spoke warmly of their vision of a Church that was doing well and was ready to meet the challenges of the twenty-first century.

After a few interventions, Archbishop George looked across at me and said: 'Jayne, would you like to say anything?' I remember looking at him squarely in the face and saying, with some passion:

'I think you must belong to a different Church to the one I belong to, Archbishop. I'm sorry, but I fear we have our fingers in our ears and our hands over our eyes, and we're not prepared to hear or see the truth. The Church I belong to is losing 50,000 children a week (according to figures from the Christian Research Association), its buildings are falling down, its clergy are depressed, we have lost the respect of the nation and yet you all seem to think it's all doing fine!'

Naturally taken aback at this outburst, Archbishop George looked around the room. He then said the only thing a typical Anglican could say in the circumstances: 'I think we need a cup of tea!'.

Oh, there's so much more I could say about our Council meetings – but that too would be the subject of another book.

The exchange did at least prompt me to start the Listening Programme. This I did by working with various contacts around the country who helped me set up and run a variety of Focus Groups, mostly with the non-churched and those who rarely attended church. I also tried to talk to loyal church members about what they thought our priorities should be. Even back then in 1999 'Talking About Human Sexuality' came up as the thing we did most frequently, although nearly every group I spoke to agreed that 'Mission' should in fact be our top priority.

Sadly, no one at the time ever seemed to see the obvious link between the two – many still don't.

I eventually presented The Listening Programme findings to Council and was given ten minutes to do so at the end of a meeting. Frustrated, I galloped through my 30-minute presentation. After I finished there was complete silence, and then a certain Archbishop looked up at me and said: 'You've spoken to the wrong people, Jayne, people don't really think this.'

I was gutted – were we really so in the dark about what was going on in the 'real world'?

'Oh yes they do,' came a voice from around the table, 'we just don't want to admit it!'

Ultimately my work would become the *Restoring Hope in Our Church* project, which would bring together all seven UK mission agencies to create a resource pack that aimed to equip parishes to recognise and address the challenges they faced. We provided a video, presented by the (then) Revd Canon Dr Tom Wright and headed by Archbishop Rowan Williams. In fact, it was shot at the start of his very first day in office, which I thought highly apt as it meant his first words were to the whole of the Church. It also gave an honest appraisal of the challenges facing the Church, set out by a range of senior Anglican voices – including Archbishop David Hope, Bishop Michael Nazir-Ali, the (then) Revd Stephen Cottrell and Dr Christina Baxter. I was pleased it also urged people to pray.

But I jump ahead.

———— • ————

Plans for the Millennium were in full force. The only problem was that it was by no means certain that there would be a Christian moment within the formal celebrations to mark the 2000th birthday of Christ himself. Long hard conversations with the government had not borne any fruit.

Extremely concerned about this, I remember waking in

the middle of the night with what seemed an obvious idea – we should ask the people! I therefore wrote to Archbishop George and explained that for a few hundred pounds we could conduct a YouGov survey, which would ask those who were planning to stay at home and watch the Millennium Dome celebrations at midnight whether they wanted a moment to mark the birth of Christ. My thinking was that it would primarily be the older generations who were most likely to be at home that night and glued to their TV sets.

The results came back convincingly clear. I remember them slowly printing out on the Lambeth fax machine (thank goodness for faxes) and the sheer excitement of seeing the research figures.

No 10 were not well pleased, but how could they argue with what the people wanted?

So, it was agreed that the Archbishop of Canterbury would lead the nation in the Lord's Prayer at midnight.

———•———

The first half of 1999 had been a whirlwind, and I needed a break. My finances were low (well, to be precise, non-existent) and I had no idea where such a holiday would come from. As it happened I was to spend it on a little boat, the U-Go-I-Go, sailing around the West Coast of Scotland. Idyllic. The only unusual thing was that my hosts were a lovely elderly Christian couple, introduced to me by Gill Brentford, who would use this time to minister and pray with me.

Rosanne and Henry had been involved with the Christian healing ministry for most of their lives. Indeed, Rosanne was herself first baptised in the gifts of the Holy Spirit back in the 1970s and, it seemed, she had a particular gift of praying for healing. She'd had a very clear word that she was to invite me to stay with them, even though they had retired from their ministry some years earlier. And so together we went through my past and prayed into all the significant events.

It was an unusual experience. Waking each morning to the extraordinary beauty of the West Coast of Scotland, often with a Tall Ship in sight, while also reliving some of the most painful moments of my life. But I was certain Mr God was with us, and as such it was a blessed and rejuvenating time.

It was thanks to Rosanne that I gained a deep passion and respect for scripture. I remember her asking me to fetch her Bible once, and on picking it up I realised that she had read *all* of it. Up till that point I – like many evangelicals – had focused primarily on the New Testament. In fact, I had never really ventured far into the major – or minor – Old Testament prophets. But Rosanne had studied them all and had underlined key verses which proved it. I soon found myself doing the same. I learnt so much from her, particularly how to pray into scripture and how to apply it to past events as well as current situations. It all made a very deep and profound impression on me.

The one tiny shadow that hung over me during these extraordinary weeks was that I knew I had to preach my first sermon at the end of it all, and I felt hopelessly ill-equipped to do this.

I had no one to blame but myself. I had had quite heated words with our vicar, John, one evening after a sermon in which he had said his role was to enable us all to shine like diamonds. I had asked him how that could possibly be true when I was being asked to lead things on a national level, where I often had to speak, but that I had never yet been invited to speak in my own church.

A few days later he asked if I'd like to preach. I remember him sending me the title 'How to Hold onto Hope?' and the reading 1 Timothy 1:1-16 and thinking that I just couldn't see the link between the two. I decided the best thing to do was to ask the three people whose sermons I enjoyed the most how they prepared to preach. This yielded some fascinating advice – including 'focus on the right springboard at the start and the rest will just follow'.

I spent ages praying over the text, and finally felt I had 'a word' that I hoped would be a blessing to those who perhaps, like me, had been going through a tough time. On the day of the service, I fasted and prayed, and felt that there were likely to be three groups of people who might need some prayer afterwards. I met with John before the service and tried to say as much. He, understandably (given he'd never heard me preach before) said: 'Let's wait and see, Jayne.'

I was so nervous. I can remember my sweaty palms and racing heartbeat, and the awful feeling of finishing and going back to my seat, wondering whether it had made any sense to anyone. John got up on stage, visibly moved, and asked if I would join him there to share the three groups I had mentioned earlier. I did so, then went down to my place while the worship band sang a song.

I closed my eyes and pleaded: 'Please, Lord, please let there be at least one person who wants prayer.' I was scared to open them. What if I'd got this wrong? I could hear movement, but still didn't want to open my eyes. I moved to the side by the wall, and then heard an even louder sound of chairs being moved. I opened my eyes and remember sliding down the wall into a little heap on the floor. It seemed like the whole church had come forward for prayer that evening. There was no one left to pray with anyone – just hundreds of people standing at the front in response.

John tried to deal with it as best he could. But it was a night like no other, for which I thank and praise God. It was absolutely nothing to do with me, and all to do with the grace of God at work.

At the heart of the sermon was a message of just how safe we are in God's hands, but that we need to learn to let go of our safety nets so that we can truly know how safe we were. The picture I had was of a guy hanging by his fingers off a cliff edge, desperately frightened that he was going to fall. However, his wrists were actually being held by Jesus, who had a good hold of him, but he had no idea of this as he was trying to hang on in his own strength.

It was a message to me and, I felt, a message to the Church.[1]

It did cause a bit of a problem though. What had I done that other preachers hadn't? It was a question I understood that the leaders were debating. I realised now that I had become a threat.

A few months later I got a letter from the Revd John Coles, the then Leader of New Wine, to ask if I would like to preach at his church in North Finchley. The invite made me smile as it said I could bring my own 'ministry team'. I had a few dear friends who prayed with me – would that do, I wondered?

That sermon was also memorable, but for a very different reason.

I was naturally keen to give them a rousing message, one that would get them all inspired and – I hoped – result in an invite to speak at New Wine. I say this, knowing how it reads, but the truth is that I was terribly keen for lay women to be embraced by the New Wine movement. We desperately needed more role models who weren't just the wives of all the New Wine leaders.

The only problem was that I didn't have 'a word'. I prayed, and I fasted, and I prayed some more. I started to panic. Nothing.

[1] The whole sermon can be read in *The Sixth Times Book of Best Sermons*

Preach it, Sister!

Nada. Zilch. It was now Saturday night and I was due to preach at the morning service and then again in the evening. I could give the readings when I arrived thankfully.

And then it came. An incredibly tough word, about how competitive churches could be and how many yearned to show how 'successful' they were. It centred on me asking what had been the greatest problem that Jesus had had to confront his disciples about? All the answers seemed to point to their competitiveness. Who got to sit nearest to him, or who spent most time with him.

My heartfelt belief was that those of us in 'successful churches' needed to learn to go out and serve. That our large mega churches needed to get alongside those that were really struggling, and instead of trying to take them over, should just ask them how they could best help.

It didn't go down very well. I could feel the coldness in the room, but I kept on going. I stayed for lunch with John and Anne, and then went through it all again in the evening. John came up to me afterwards and said that he understood the heart of my message, but he didn't think his church was ready to hear it yet. Not ready to hear it? So, what was it going to take for them to be ready I thought? That was the whole point – they were too comfortable, too cosy, too safe.

The only saving grace was that a lovely lady, who explained she'd been praying for me, came up as I was leaving and said: 'Take heart Jayne, you're not the only visiting preacher to have given such a word!'

———•———

So, I now had a reputation of being a bit dangerous in the eyes of some of my evangelical friends.

In fact, I began to sense that there was something fundamentally different between many of us.

The truth is that God had broken my heart over the state

of the Church of England. Yet instead of hitting it, belittling it and making it the butt of jokes – which many seemed to enjoy doing in their sermons – I wanted to pray for it. I therefore got increasingly upset with many evangelical leaders over their attitude towards the Church. It was never said, but I assumed it was to do with the fact that they thought that many felt 'they had the gift of the Holy Spirit' and that they thought that most of the rest of the Church was involved in a form of 'dead religion'. The thing was, I had spent time with many non-evangelicals and I could sense the depth of their faith – it was just in a different form. Yes of course there were things that I found difficult in the way they worshipped – just as they found with me.

Yet we managed to see and respect the Christ in each other.

Looking back, I recognise now that this was the start of me realising that the evangelical wing of the Church was not always right about everything, and that many held certain stances on issues that were causing deep pain and division. Such as the role of women, and of course sexuality.

But there were problems on both 'sides'. Sitting as I did on the Board of Mission, I realised there was a deep dislike of anything to do with Holy Trinity Brompton. I couldn't believe that the national body tasked with mission did not have any links with Alpha, and I frequently said as much.

I tried to set up various meetings that would bring the differing parties together, but they never seemed to bear much fruit. The deep-seated prejudice – on both sides – was just too great.

———•———

At the same time, I started to try and build bridges with the large evangelical para-church groups.

Joel Edwards, the General Director of the Evangelical Alliance, became a firm friend and a member of my Prayer Net. He was the first to take me out to lunch and say: 'Now, Jayne, how can we best serve and support you? I'm assuming everyone else wants a piece of you, and wants you to help push their agenda, but please know I see my role as being here for you!'

I could have hugged him – in fact, I think I did.

———•———

My dear Scottish friend Rosanne, believing I needed more 'prayer cover', introduced me to the Lydia Prayer Network. She was particularly keen for me to meet a close friend of hers, Olga, who had been Lord Mountbatten's private secretary during WWII. Olga was formidable. She herself had the most amazing faith journey, in which Maria von Trapp had played a significant part.

I first met Olga at the 1999 National Prayer Breakfast in London. It was not the best of meetings, as I clearly remember the look of disappointment on her face when she was introduced to me. Somehow, I know I just didn't meet her expectations of the person God was going to use 'to shake the Church of England'. But we soon became firm friends, and thanks to her a group of Regional Lydia Leaders were convened to meet and pray with me every three months or so.

It was thanks to these women that I met another influential prayer warrior, Julie Anderson from Prayer for the Nations. She in turn then introduced me to Cindy Jacobs, Anne Graham Lotz and John Mulinde – all larger-than-life characters who were involved in the international prayer network scene.

Indeed, every contact seemed to lead to another, and within months I found myself discovering parts of the international evangelical church that I never knew even existed.

CHAPTER EIGHT

Deliver Us from Evil ...

September 1999

My first encounter with Kerry was unforgettable.

She was by far the most significant international contact I ever made – an Australian woman living in South Africa who quickly became my mentor and friend. Indeed, Kerry taught me more about the nature of my calling than anyone else I've ever met. She had the most extraordinary prophetic gifting and was recognised as a 'Prophet' by many evangelical networks around the world. What was quite ironic was that this was even the case amongst those who were not so keen on women in leadership, such as the Assemblies of God, where she was frequently asked to lead leaders' training days.

During the latter half of my first year on Council, Kerry visited the UK and was invited to lead an evening on prophecy at our church. I'd not heard of her before, but she had certainly created quite a buzz amongst my friends. I was told that under no circumstances should I miss this event. However, it was on the same day as a particularly arduous Council meeting, and the last thing I decided I wanted to do was to go to yet another church meeting. So, I started to head home.

Something en route made me relent and arriving late, I slipped into a chair at the back of the hall. Kerry had already started preaching and I was finding it hard to concentrate as the frustrations of that day's Council meeting were still fresh in my mind. Suddenly she stopped, pointed directly across the room at me and said: 'You've got a big mouth!' There were roars of laughter as people, turning, realised who she was speaking to. I went bright red and could feel a flush of anger fuelled by embarrassment rise up within me. This was all I needed.

'You've got a big mouth! You go into meetings, you swear you're not going to say anything, and yet you just can't keep quiet. You have to speak what is in your heart, and you can't understand why they don't see the things that you see and hear the things you hear. But fear not, God is with you, and you are going to bring hope to many – to so, so many people, right across the world.'

Everyone fell deathly quiet – unlike Kerry, most present knew I was a member of the Archbishops' Council (even if few understood what that meant) and so realised – even if she didn't – who she was talking about. It was her hallmark I would later understand – God would reveal to her something so utterly personal about an individual that they'd then be open to receiving the word she had from God for them.

I sat in my chair bewildered. How on earth could she know that? It was all so true! Just that morning I had decided that I was not going to say anything in Council. In my mind I had said more than enough over the past few months and had caused far too many waves. But try as I might, I just couldn't keep quiet – the burden to speak was too strong. To try to manage this I had taken to sitting between two new Council friends with whom I would work closely over the next few years, Dr Philip Giddings and Bishop Michael Nazir-Ali, so that we could swap short notes about what was going on. But that only seemed to increase my desire to speak – not diminish it.

At the end of the meeting I went up to speak to Kerry and thanked her. I explained that I knew she hadn't a clue who I was, but that due to some rather extraordinary circumstances I was on something called the Church of England's Archbishops' Council. I then said something that was to become a bit of a catchphrase for me – that if she ever needed someone to 'carry her bags' I would be delighted to do so, as I was keen to learn as much as I could from her.

I realised that this must have seemed a rather pathetic thing to say – the whole Church wanted to spend time with her. However, she took my home-made card and said she would pray about it.

A few months later I was woken by an early morning phone call. I looked at my clock – 6.30 a.m. – and immediately panicked. It must be bad news from home, who else would be calling at that hour in the morning? I stumbled out of bed to get to the phone as quickly as I could, braced for the worst, and on lifting the receiver heard the click of a long-distance call.

'Jayne, I've been praying. God's put you on my heart, He's put the Church of England on my heart, and He's put the United Kingdom on my heart. Would you like to come over and spend some time with me here in South Africa?'

Kerry must have forgotten the time difference I realised as I endeavoured to get my head in gear. I couldn't really believe what she was saying, and I was still trying to recover from the fact it wasn't bad news. South Africa? How on earth was I going to afford to go there? I said I'd pray about it.

We were now in a new millennium, and the international Prayer Networks were buzzing with a new video that had been produced by George Otis Junior, who'd created an inspirational resource to encourage his intercessors. *Transformations* documented the incredible stories of what God was doing around the world when small groups of Christians met together to pray. Communities were being transformed, prisons emptied, crops multiplied – and all because of prayer.

Deliver Us from Evil

It was so exciting – God seemed to be doing a 'new thing' and moving in such power across the world. The result was that everyone wanted to know what they should do to be part of the action.

SOMA[1] – a global network of charismatic Anglicans, headed by the Revd Don Brewin – decided to host a conference to determine the core lessons from the video. They invited the international leaders involved with making the video to speak, and all the senior Anglican charismatics they knew around the world to attend, including myself. It was to be held in Cape Town later that October.

I knew that that I was meant to go – which meant I knew I could also go and visit Kerry. But how was I going to fund it? At the time I was literally living off my Archbishops' Council travel expenses plus a few sporadic gifts from friends, and there was no way I could afford the plane fare. So, we prayed.

The next Sunday after the service I was approached by Charlie Colchester, a dear friend from church who had started CARE with Lyndon Bowring. 'Jayne, I think you're meant to be going somewhere, so I want to give you some money to cover the trip.' I thanked him and explained that it was quite a journey that would require several flights, but he just smiled and nodded.

——— • ———

Now it's time to share something that not all readers are going to find easy to read or understand, but I'd ask you to just 'go with it' for now please. It's as important part of my story, and one that I feel needs to be 'brought into the light' as it shows what so many of us have been put through.

For some time, I had been plagued during my prayer times by a gagging feeling around my throat. It seemed to come out

[1] Sharing of Ministries Abroad

of the blue, but only after I had got onto the Archbishops' Council. At first, I thought it was just psychosomatic given all the stress I had been under, but the feeling started to get stronger as I prayed more, and so I began to feel somewhat 'under attack'.

I didn't really know what to do about it. I knew it sounded all rather strange, and I was loath to share it with anyone. I certainly had never heard of anyone else experiencing this before. I interpreted it as a spiritual attempt to silence me and began to consider what the cause might be.

My first thought was that I had this enormous secret from my past, and that for some reason I was being tormented or held back because I hadn't been open about it with the Church. I decided I needed to share my rather unique story with someone in authority who I trusted, and who I thought would understand – so I approached Bishop Michael Turnbull, the then Bishop of Durham.

Bishop Michael had become a good friend, and a great encourager to me on Council. The very Council that he himself had been instrumental in forming. The only time I ever remember us disagreeing was over a proposal regarding the future number of bishops in the House of Lords. I argued that we ought to recognise the wider Christian representation already available in the House, and that we didn't need 26 bishops. The bishops, perhaps unsurprisingly, did not agree.

I asked Bishop Michael if I could visit him in Durham as I had something very private and confidential to talk to him about, which he kindly agreed to and duly invited me to stay. Auckland Castle is breath taking – do go and visit if you can, it's certainly worth the tour. Be warned though, it's enormous – I remember thinking that my bathroom was larger than the whole of my London flat.

Bishop Michael served me supper, and I launched in with my rather nervous account of the fact that I had a past, and I thought it was important – just in case the press got to hear of it – for someone within the senior echelons of the Church to know about it. I explained that I believed I was now healed after a lot of emotional healing prayer, and that fortunately I had no desires at all – for anyone. In fact, I explained, I felt that I was being called to be single for my time on Council.

Bishop Michael was so gracious, kind and pastoral in his response. He must have been wondering what I was going to say to him, but he never showed it. He said I was very brave for talking about it all, and that he felt privileged I'd chosen to entrust him with it – we both knew why I had chosen to do so with him. I let out a sigh of relief, surely now the gagging feeling would go – but it didn't.

So, I arrived a Kerry's – with a very infected big toe to boot. This was thanks to an ingrowing toe-nail which had been severely impacted by the change in pressure during my various plane journeys. Kerry and her husband Geoff lived on a farm in the middle of the bush, somewhere near Gariep Dam. The nearest city was Bloemfontein, and we spent much of our first two days going backwards and forward to the doctors. The whole escapade meant that sadly I wasn't able to walk far and so instead of going out to explore, we stayed at home and talked.

I was put in the Annex Suite – the most beautiful 'country style' bedroom with everything a guest could ever have hoped for. Kerry certainly knew the meaning of hospitality. But the first night I had the most awful nightmares, and for one of the first times in my life I felt incredibly scared. I couldn't explain it – it was as if a huge dread had wrapped itself around me. It was most definitely spiritual – that's all I knew. Kerry asked if I wanted to move back into the main house, and I gratefully said yes. The only place it turned out I felt safe was in a small bed just outside their own bedroom. This was better, but something was still not right. The third evening we talked about it in some depth, and I eventually told them about the gagging feeling that I had been experiencing.

Kerry looked at Geoff, and then proceeded to tell me that she had felt I needed some spiritual deliverance. He agreed to stay and pray quietly 'in the spirit' in the corner of the room, to give us some prayer cover, whilst she ministered to me. I was naturally nervous, but I knew there was nothing to worry about as I was in safe and experienced hands.

That evening was one of the longest in my life – or so it felt. Kerry would start to pray for me, and then I would feel something happen in my throat and I would want to cough up whatever it was. I found myself constantly gagging and trying to speak – but something had a hold of my tongue. I felt utterly paralysed and couldn't get out any of the words she wanted me to say, namely 'the blood of Jesus sets me free'. I had no idea what was happening but believed that a whole horde of demons were being cast out of me. This tied in with a word Rosanne had had for me once, where she felt I was to be a modern-day Mary Magdalene – from whom seven spirits were cast out.

After about three hours I asked if I could go to the bathroom. I needed a break. I still remember the utter shock of looking in the mirror and seeing my eye sockets, which had become quite dark and were covered in deep red speckles. I rushed back to the lounge and asked what on earth this meant. Kerry explained it was the sign of witchcraft. I gulped, and we continued with the ministry.

The red spots stayed with me for three days. I was worried they would still be there for the SOMA conference in Cape Town but luckily, they had receded by then. I know this may all sound terribly strange to some readers – but the truth is that this sort of deliverance happens a lot in charismatic evangelical churches, and if you're part of one it all seems quite 'normal'. We worship a supernatural God and are therefore taught to expect supernatural things to happen.

Deliver Us from Evil

The key thing was that the gagging sensation had gone – although my throat was incredibly sore.

————————•—•————————

I came back to England and reflected on my time with Kerry. She was someone I trusted completely and knew had my best interests at heart. She had taught me so much – not least how best to pray for people when you have a prophetic gifting, which she had recognised within me. I remember asking her one evening when she had asked me to minister alongside her 'How did she do it?' She just smiled at me and said with her very strong Australian accent: 'Why, Jayne, I just pray for them with all the love I possibly can in my heart. JUST LOVE them! God will do the rest!'

JUST LOVE!

It was simple – I've never looked back.

I believed – as she did – that she needed to come back to the UK, so I suggested her as a keynote speaker for a launch conference of a new ministry I was involved with, *Called to Business*. This was aimed at Christians in the City of London who wanted fellowship and prayer, as well as some in-depth teaching about things they believed they were spiritually dealing with at work, such as freemasonry or 'mammon'. It was agreed that Kerry would be a speaker alongside another South African, Steve Worrall-Clare, who was an expert in Freemasonry, as well as David Pawson and others.

The conference – held in the rather grand Gibson Hall in the heart of the City of London – was a great success. Well that is so long as you don't count one of the speeches. Following a highly sexist talk, I had to get up on stage and apologise to all the women present, and indeed anyone else who had been offended by what they had heard.

However, it was during this conference that I started to learn in detail about the spiritual roots of Freemasonry. In fact, as Steve Worrall-Clare was speaking I began to feel another weird sensation – a painful stabbing through the centre of my forehead, just between my eyebrows. I was reliably informed by him that this was my 'third eye'. It was thanks to Steve that I met his UK associate Derek Roberts, from Freedom Ministries International. Derek in turn invited me to attend his 'Freedom from Freemasonry' deliverance courses – so I could learn more and be prayed for.

———•———

It might be worth explaining that the attitude I had during this highly unusual chapter in my life was to have the courage to walk through any door that God seemed to open for me, as I felt I was on a very steep learning curve. I also desperately wanted to be free of anything that might hinder me from doing the work I felt called to, and the unusual physical manifestations that I experienced whilst praying led me to believe that there were indeed such things at work. I decided that my past troubles regarding my sexuality were probably all linked to this too and realised that as well as emotional healing – which I was still pursuing – I might also need some more deliverance.

I was however very nervous about being 'found out' as a 'senior Anglican' in these circles, especially when receiving prayer ministry. At first, I thought that the best thing to do was to go abroad so as to be able to participate in some emotional healing seminars led by Lin Button. Lin worked closely with Leanne Payne, and soon became a form of spiritual counsellor to me.

Anyway, emboldened by my experiences with Kerry, I decided to book into a conference in Stroud with Freedom Ministries International and so took the risk of 'being seen'. I soon began to realise that nobody had a clue who I was anyway, and that I need never have worried. That said, it was always difficult to answer the question 'What do you do?', which I tried to avoid being asked.

Deliver Us from Evil

The conference seemed to be going quite well. We were gradually working our way through the various orders of Freemasonry and praying for freedom from any curses associated with each level. Around midday we broke for lunch, and I went off to find a sandwich. On my return, a couple of ladies asked if they could pray with me, and I gratefully agreed explaining about the stabbing pain in my forehead. We started praying, but nothing seemed to happen.

An elderly gentleman called Robert, the 'senior prayer minister', approached and asked if he could join us. I agreed and bowed my head. He then said something, which to this day still makes my stomach churn: 'I see you have the Spirit of Man on you, Jayne'. The only problem was that it did literally make my stomach churn. I was violently sick – into a bucket that was hastily brought from behind the curtains (they were evidently quite prepared for this form of spiritual manifestation). I've never been so sick in my life – it felt like I was bringing up everything from the very core of me. I was stunned, shaken and perplexed. What on earth had just happened?

I suppose that is where I first began to believe that one could be delivered of homosexual spirits. 'The Spirit of Man', which Robert had seen was, I believed, the reason for my attraction to women. The word 'homosexuality' was never used, but I knew that's what he had meant. Interestingly though, after years of severe pelvic pain and heavy bleeding I suddenly found that my periods were more manageable. I saw it as a sign and believed I had been a recipient of a work of grace.

Importantly, it was after this incident that I believed I could be set free from my unwanted homosexual desires – if only we prayed hard enough, with the right authority and insight. Sadly, it was to take me several more years before I realised that no amount of prayer, no matter how fervent or heartfelt, could change something that is part of the unique and marvellous work of creation that makes me, me. Our greatest challenge is to accept and celebrate who we have been uniquely created to be and know that we are each loved equally.

It was thanks to Kerry's trip to the UK that I met another extraordinary woman, Olave, who was to become a close friend and my greatest source of support for the remainder of my time on Council.

Olave hosted the *Prayer Programme* on Premier Radio and was keen to invite Kerry for an interview so she could quiz her about what she felt was happening spiritually in Britain. I'd not met Olave before, but we clicked immediately. She was an old friend of Rosanne's and Olga's, and well known and loved by the Lydia Prayer Network. Her namesake was her Godmother, Olave Baden Powell, with whom she had lived for several years when she had first moved to London from Africa.

Kerry suggested to Olave that she should interview me too, which Olave duly arranged to do. It was after we had recorded this interview – my first ever radio programme – that Olave suggested that we might want to meet together to pray. She explained that she has been seeking a prayer partner, following the death of her previous dear friend. I was so grateful – finally I had someone who felt called to walk alongside me through all that I was going through on Council and in the world beyond. Plus, this wonderful new friend was an absolute giant in intercession.

The next few years were much the same. I found myself travelling to some fascinating places and meeting some utterly amazing people. The most memorable was my 2001 trip to Israel with Olga for a Reconciliation Conference between Jews and Germans, led by the Sisters of Darmstadt.

Deliver Us from Evil

It was an extremely demanding trip – for so many different reasons. I was confronted head on with the horrors of the Holocaust, having forged a close bond with one of the key note speakers, Janina, who was one of the few remaining survivors of the Kraków Ghetto. Her brother had been instrumental in smuggling out the research plans to help create 'the bomb' and she had had to watch him be slowly tortured to death. This was Janina's first trip 'home', and she was understandably overcome by it all. She had hesitated to tell people about her ordeals, suffering as so many survivors do from the guilt of being one of the ones who 'made it'. She had lost her faith, which I told her was completely understandable, and for some reason she then felt safe confiding in me.

She had brought with her a list of names of all the children she had known who had been born and then died in the Ghetto, and who sadly were therefore unknown and unremembered to those outside. Her hope was to present the names to the Children's Memorial at Yad Vashem, the Holocaust Memorial Centre in Jerusalem, so they would never be forgotten. There was to be an Act of Remembrance there on the final day of our conference, and I suggested that that would probably be the best time for us to do something.

On the last day we duly arrived for the ceremony and were ushered into the Memorial Hall – a large dark room lit only by an eternal flame. The floor was covered with a bronze relief of Europe and had the names of all the Death Camps and the number of people who had died emboldened in relief. The surrounding balcony was packed to capacity, and I could see there was little way we could do anything meaningful.

Being taller than most, I put my arms around Janina who was virtually half my height, and gently manoeuvred us towards the front of the balcony. Recognising her as the main speaker from the day before those around us parted to let us through. Her harrowing account had been one of the most memorable speeches in the programme, and the whole assembly had stood as one in silence afterwards to mark their deep respect for her. Clapping had seemed so utterly inappropriate.

She got out her list and asked me to help her read it out loud, there in the hall as a tribute. My Polish is non-existent, but, somehow, I found the ability to pronounce these dear children's names correctly with her as a hush descended on all those around us. Tears started streaming down my face, and I could feel an inner scream of 'Why, Oh Lord?' rise up.

After the remembrance service had finished, we all filed out into the warm April sunshine. I could see Janina was upset and went over to comfort her, knowing how much what she had just done must have meant to her. She took my hand and asked: 'Jayne, will you come back in with me?'

The hall couldn't have felt more different. It was just the two of us in this vast dimly lit space that felt almost oppressive in its solemnness and silence. Gone were the hordes of noisy people, replaced instead with the sound of our footsteps as we made our way to the middle of the balcony. Standing directly opposite the eternal flame, I put my arm round Janina not knowing what to say.

'Can you pray please, Jayne?'

Pray?! What on earth was there to say? I scrabbled around in my head for something kind and loving to say, but nothing seemed to fit the enormity of what we were facing. So, I just said what was in my heart – it's what I've always done. It's what I will continue to do for the rest of my life.

'Lord, we don't understand. We don't know "why" and we want to know "why?"... Where were you in all of this? Why did you let this all happen?'

We both started to cry. I had absolutely no idea what to do next.

Then suddenly the doors were flung open and bright light streamed in. Dozens of young school children came running in, laughing and shouting at the fun of being in such a dark place. They must have been only about five or six years old, the boys with their little skull caps and payots[2] and the girls in their dresses. Janina turned towards them, beamed and whispered: 'That's why, Jayne'.

I know it isn't a full answer, but it was enough for her at that moment in time, thank God.

We went back to our hotel, where I found Olga already back in our room. She had kindly offered to share with me so that I could keep the price of the trip down. I recognised that this must have come at an enormous cost to her personally – sharing her space with someone after so many years of being a widow must have been very challenging. I must also admit for my part, sharing with a rather deaf octogenarian was not that easy for me either. We had completely different biological clocks for a start – I was a night owl, and she would rise at the crack of dawn.

Needing space after what had been an emotional day, I went up onto the roof of the hotel to pray.

'Lord, please help. I'm not sure if I can do this. I'm going to be honest and say I'm finding it really difficult to cope with Olga', I mumbled. 'I mean – she doesn't hear a word I say, she doesn't remember a word I say, and no matter how much I try to love her it just bounces right off!'

I still remember the laughter ringing in my ears.

I was confused, this was the last thing I needed. 'Dearest Jayne,' came the response, 'I know *exactly* how you feel – *you* don't hear a word I say, *you* don't remember a word I say, and no matter how much I try to love *you* it just bounces right off!'

Touché. I'd learnt my lesson.

The next time I returned to Israel was with Canon Andrew White, when I was working as an adviser to the International Centre for Reconciliation in Coventry. Back then he was working

[2] Curly sidelocks of hair as worn by Orthodox Jews

alongside a colleague, a certain Justin Welby, whose work focused more on Nigeria than the Middle East. Bishop Colin Bennetts had asked a small group of us to review the Centre's work to ensure we had the right structures in place to cope with the large-scale growth in workload and finances that they were experiencing. This would eventually lead to the recommendation for us to set up the Foundation for Reconciliation and Relief in the Middle East, which I worked with Andrew White and Lord Carey to do.

The way I'd best sum up Andrew White's work in the Middle East is that he acts as a human telephone between the various sides of a conflict, where none are able or willing to talk to each other. All sides trusted him. We also worked with a group of religious leaders, including the Chief Rabbis, the Patriarchs and various Palestinian Sheikhs to understand reality of the situation on the ground. It wasn't the ideal place for a woman, but I was always treated with the utmost respect.

In fact, a few years on I would take my mother and Kerry too, and together with Andrew and others we would meet Yasser Arafat. It was an unforgettable meeting which ended with him offering my mother five camels for me! 'Only five?' I said jokingly, before adding, 'Rais,[3] can I possibly ask you something?' He nodded. Summoning up all my courage, I said: 'I wonder what you think God makes of all this – I mean, there is so much pain on both sides?' He looked at me for a moment, then shrugged his shoulders and walked away – an old man who I felt just wanted to go home.

———◄•►———

Thanks to Olave, Olga, Julie Anderson and others I met countless other international evangelical speakers over the next few years, many of whom I would ask to pray for me – hoping they would be able to 'sort me out'. From YWAM leaders in

[3] The Arabic term used to address rulers of Arab states in the Middle East

Argentina to the Arnotts of 'Toronto blessing' fame in Canada. Thanks to Lin Button I also started to attend meetings run by Leanne Payne and Andy Comiskey, as well as others led by Lisa and Chris Guinness. All these had the simple aim of trying to help those of us suffering from ungodly sexual desires. I must admit I felt quite exposed sitting in these meetings, and only managed a couple if truth be told – it was all too public for me.

So, I continued with my bespoke journey of emotional healing and spiritual deliverance – trusting I'd meet the right people to pray for me at the right time. There were moments though when I felt that people were attempting to cast out the very core of me – I would find myself coughing and then realise that the whole of me was trying to 'come up'. In many ways I suppose that this was quite true – you can't possibly cast out homosexuality as if it's an add-on. It IS you.

It is the very heart of you, quite literally.

——— • ———

The years on Council began to mount up.

Towards the end of my first three-year term I was asked if I would stay and serve for another three years. I felt that six was the maximum I should do since I feared that I too was becoming too institutionalised, and so was becoming part of the problem rather than the solution.

By far the most important initiative I led was the *Restoring Hope in Our Church* project, which despite all the rumours, was not about us trying to restore our Patron, the Most Revd David Hope, to Canterbury.

Archbishop David had also become a good friend and had been more than willing to help me with the initiative. To recap, this was about bringing the UK mission agencies together to create a resource for churches that set out the core challenges we were facing as a Church, encouraging them to pray and form discipleship groups, and urging them to agree a mission plan that addressed their specific community situation. It was the fulfilment of the Listening Programme, which I had conducted to try and help the Church become more open and honest about its problems.

I had no idea how we were going to pull this off – especially given I had turned down an offer of help from the main UK Christian funder, the Jerusalem Trust, because they wanted us to sell the video pack. I truly believed it was meant to be free, and that it should be sent to every parish in the country.

Perhaps the most heart-warming miracle in all of this was the way God used my own father to underwrite the costs of the project, even though he was very ill with cancer at the time.

Archbishop David had agreed to help make a launch video that we could show at a fringe at General Synod, and so I went up to York for the day to film him and parts of the Minster. Sitting in his study, I asked if he could possibly pray for us before we started the filming as there was so much at stake. We sat silently and prayed. Much to my surprise I found myself going immediately very hot – which for me was a sign of the Holy Spirit at work. I looked up at Archbishop David and saw he was smiling – we both knew this project would somehow be surely blessed.

A couple of weeks later I was sat in an editing suite, wondering how on earth I was going to finish the film in the time we had. More critically though was the nagging question of how we were going to finance it. I could feel my phone vibrating in my pocket but left it alone – the editing time was just too precious. On the second set of rings I decided to take it – realising it might be news from my mother about my father who was awaiting test results following his chemotherapy treatment.

'I'm just wondering who I make the cheque out to?' came a voice I didn't recognise. I asked who I was speaking to and was informed it was a call on behalf of something called the Garfield Weston Foundation. 'Gosh, that's really very kind of you,' I said, 'do you mind saying how you heard about the project?' 'Oh, we've decided to provide matched funding,' the lady responded. I was now totally confused – matched funding, with whom? The speaker continued: 'It follows the recent request we've had from the Laing Foundation. We were told this would be a very good way of showing our support for the new Archbishop of Canterbury.'

I was stunned, I'd no idea they had been approached – I understand now that I have Sir Ewan Harper of the Lambeth Partners to thank, who had obviously been in touch on my behalf. I said how grateful I was, and nervously asked if I might know how much they were thinking of giving?

'Oh, haven't you heard? We've each agreed to fund the project £25,000!'

I nearly dropped the phone. Fifty thousand pounds! In one instant, the budget was met – a quick phone call from someone I didn't know and had never asked. I nearly hadn't even taken their call.

I stood bewildered in the staircase and found myself shouting 'Thank you! Thank you! Thank you!' My phone started to ring again – it was my mother. My father had just been given the all clear. His cancer had gone – the doctors were amazed. I choked up and said I would call her back.

Miracles happen. No, I know they don't happen all the time, but they do definitely happen!

CHAPTER NINE

It's Raining Men!

October 2003

We stood staring into the gaping missile crater. Although it was mid-October, it was still relatively warm however I suddenly felt chilled to the bone. The realities of war were very sobering.

We were standing in the grounds of the huge Armenian monastery of Gandzasar in the heart of the disputed territory of Nagorno-Karabakh. It felt like I was in a set from Lord of the Rings – this thirteenth-century cathedral, believed to house the relics of St John the Baptist and his father, Zechariah, was perched high on a rock and stood guard over the whole surrounding region. It was their equivalent of Canterbury Cathedral, housing the spiritual heart and soul of Nagorno-Karabakh.

The Archbishop of Artsakh (as Nagorno-Karabakh is colloquially known) was addressing our small group, which was led by our host, Baroness Caroline Cox. We were an unlikely bunch. A husband, wife and son who together formed one of the richest families in America, accompanied by their bodyguard, best friend and theologian, a retired clergy couple, Caroline's eldest son – and me.

I was still pinching myself. A couple of weeks earlier I hadn't even heard of Nagorno-Karabakh, let alone understood its turbulent war-torn history as an Armenian enclave within Azerbaijan. I had only just learnt that Armenia was the first ever Christian nation, thanks to the witness of St Gregory. Nor had I realised that the mountain whose picture I had taken when visiting his cell on our way out of Yerevan was in fact Mount Ararat, where Noah's Ark is traditionally believed to have come to rest.

You might not be surprised to hear that I first met Caroline in some rather unusual circumstances. I had been invited to the launch of her latest book, *The West, Islam and Islamism*, in late June 2003 in the House of Lords. Although busy, I had decided to go on the basis that I would hopefully get a synopsis of the book in the speeches, which would then save me the time of having to read it.

You can imagine my horror therefore when I arrived in the reception room to find a group of twenty theologians and scholars all sat round a large table, waiting to discuss the book. This was not the typical launch drinks party I was used to. Caroline opened by saying she was grateful for everyone making time to attend, and that she proposed going around the table so that everyone could give their account of what they had thought about the book and its implications for the UK.

Fortunately, I was sat on the far side of the table, and so had a bit of time to gather my thoughts. I was the only other female in the room, and as always one of the youngest. I felt terribly out of my depth, and had that sickening feeling of not having completed my homework in time (an unusual thing for me). I decided that honesty was the best policy, and so when it came to my turn I said:

'I'm terribly sorry, Caroline, I haven't yet had a chance to read your book. However, I recognise the importance of this subject and given I know so little about it, I've come to listen and learn.'

Caroline beamed – she responded well to honesty. A short while later I gave my excuses and explained that I had to go to a meeting at Church House. Caroline got up with me and followed me out: 'We should meet', she said. I said I'd like that very much, and then cheekily added: 'If you ever need anyone to carry your bags, please say – as there's so much I'd love to learn from you!'

'Come to Nagorno-Karabakh with me!' she immediately responded, smiling: 'I'm taking a group out in October.' Where's Nagorno-Karabakh, I wondered, and why on earth are we going there?

The problem as always was finance, although I was beginning to believe that whenever a new door opened the funds would somehow always follow through. The slight challenge this time was that we were travelling with an exceptionally rich family, which meant we weren't staying in budget hotels. They were covering Caroline's costs but, well, we couldn't expect them to do so for me.

I bought the airline ticket in faith, putting it on my credit card, and prayed. Nothing appeared to happen. Come the week before our trip I was seriously starting to panic. I was also feeling incredibly frustrated as earlier that year I had done some charity consultancy work and been paid quite well for it. Nothing too much, but enough to allow me time to relax and breathe for a few months. However, the day after I received the money I learnt that a communications company with which Olave and I were involved, *Just Connections Network*, owed an investor some funds. Realising that my sense of financial security was to be short lived, I agreed to pay off the debt with the promise that the company would pay me back shortly. They had yet to do so.

Three days before I was due to fly I received a phone call from a friend who managed a charitable trust that people could donate to if they wanted to help support me: 'Jayne, we've just received a donation of £2000 from someone for you. I just thought you'd want to know.'

I was going!

And so there I was on this rocky outcrop, looking into the hole created by an Azeri grad missile.

'It was the only one to land in our monastery grounds,' the Archbishop was explaining, 'and ironically the explosion revealed some buried ancient hatzcars,[1] which we had no idea were there. The miracle though is that no missile ever landed on the monastery. They tried hard by dropping hundreds of bombs, but every time one fell it seemed to bounce off an invisible shield!'

I knew this dear wise man was not lying. There was a real sense of holiness about him – a man who was used to spending many hours in prayer. And yet his gentle soft voice belied the fact that he had witnessed some of the most unspeakable horrors of the war.

Later that afternoon at tea he recounted how prayer had literally saved his life. Stroking his long beard and pausing to reflect, he then explained how during the war he had once woken suddenly in the middle of the night. It was in the heart of winter and bitterly cold (Armenia can drop to minus 20°C). Despite this, he felt an overwhelming urge to go down into his little chapel in the basement and pray. He had just got down on his knees when there was an almighty crash right above his head. A grad missile had fallen through the roof and was lying, unexploded, in his bed. Had he stayed there he would have been crushed to death.

I looked at him, reached over and gently touched his hand: 'Archbishop, can I ask how you feel about the Azeris now? I mean you've seen such horror and pain, with so many lives lost.'

He looked surprised at the question, then answered immediately in his thick Armenian accent:

'But I love them, Jayne. I JUST LOVE them.'

He must have seen my slight eye roll, I hadn't meant him to, but I just wasn't convinced. Now it was his turn to lean over and touch my hand: 'I love them, Jayne, because they are my enemies, and that is what we are commanded to do. The moment I stop loving them they've won!'

[1] A large Armenian style cross

Another crucial lesson in life.

JUST LOVE them. The moment you stop loving, they've won.

I promised him I would pray for peace in the region, to which he responded – taking my hand and starring straight into my eyes: 'Peace with *justice*, Jayne, otherwise it will be no peace at all!'

———◆———

It was on this trip that the plan to launch the Humanitarian Aid Relief Trust was formed, aided by our American friends. Caroline asked if I could help her set it up, and I gladly agreed to do so.

The truth was that Caroline's fearless advocacy and self-less humanitarian aid trips meant that she was often the first Westerner on the ground in various conflict areas. Faced with great need and suffering, she did whatever she could to bring some relief – often using her nursing skills. In Nagorno-Karabakh this had meant the creation of a school and a respite centre, where the disabled were treated and saved from the horrors of dying from bedsores. This was a common problem in the region, as few understood the need to keep turning patients who were not able to do so themselves in order to stop them from developing bed sores that would then get infected. In Myanmar it meant the creation of orphanages, in Sudan and East Timor taking aid … and so it went on. We even had an orphanage in Moscow for children rejected by their families because of their disabilities or because they had lost their parents, often due to alcoholism.

It was such rewarding work – but frequently heart-breaking, and very demanding for just one person to manage. The trouble was that I was doing virtually the same for Canon Andrew White's work in the Middle East too. It was to become too much – dealing with either one of these extraordinary charismatic individuals would have been enough for most, but both?

The good news is that I managed it for a season – and learnt so much from the two of them and their friends. It also formed the basis of my application to Oxford University, where I was to apply to do a course in international diplomacy, followed by research into international relations and religion.

———•———

Thanks to the generous gift, I also had enough funds to accept another invitation to visit the Latin American YWAM base in Argentina, which I had received just before I left for Armenia. The trip was being planned by a friend, Rosemary, who had been Billy Graham's private secretary. She had been asked to do some teaching on prayer and wondered if I would like to accompany her.

Again, I wasn't too sure why I was going, although ironically, I had met the YWAM leaders earlier in the summer, who had prayed for me in relation to my sexuality. Things became a lot clearer during my trip to Armenia where I learnt that the Argentinian head of the Armenian diaspora was a close friend of Caroline's, and also rather rich. She asked me if I would go and see him to give him an account of our trip, as he had been instrumental in helping to raise the funds to build all the roads we had travelled on.

So, I bought my ticket to Argentina and rather unusually felt prompted to take my violin with me. It was the violin I used only when travelling, as I was never sure where it might end up in the airplane, and the violin my father had made was far too precious to risk. This violin was to be my saving grace. What I hadn't appreciated was that we were first staying in the Outreach Centre for YWAM in Bueno Aires, and that most of their mission focused on the arts. As such they were putting together a band, which they hoped would get asked to play in local restaurants. It was a rather eclectic mix of instruments – panpipes, guitars, rain makers, even an Australian didgeridoo. Add to that a classically trained violinist ... well, at least we had great fun 'busking in the spirit'.

On the first full day I tried to call the number I'd been given to connect with Caroline's friend, Edward. Sadly, though, I couldn't even get a dialling tone – it just didn't seem to work. I was concerned; this was the first task Caroline had given me, and I didn't want to let her down. (I was to find out later I had been given all the right numbers, they just weren't all in the right order!)

The slight challenge was that there weren't many YWAMers who spoke English. We got by with miming and smiling a lot, but there were few who could help me track Edward down. So, I found the Armenian church, and asked for help there – though again neither the security guard nor the lady who came out to help spoke any English. I felt so frustrated – so near and yet so far.

I went back to the base and decided that I was obviously not meant to meet Edward. However, it seems that Mr God had other plans. There was a knock on my door, and the leader of our new band came bouncing in. 'We a gig! We a gig!' was all he could say in his pidgin English. 'That's fantastic!' I smiled enthusiastically, hoping he'd get the fact I was really excited, and held my palms upwards to ask: 'Where? When?' '*Esta noche*[2]! *Restaurante Armenio!*' Of course it was! I had just been asked to play that evening in the one and only Armenian restaurant in the whole of Buenos Aires – you couldn't write the script, could you?

And yes, of course, they knew Edward. In fact, they could give me his son's phone number.

I rang the son first thing the next morning, and he invited me to come straight over to meet him and his father at their

[2] Tonight!

headquarters. Any friend of Caroline's was a friend of theirs. The only small problem was, I had literally nothing to wear – certainly nothing suitable for a large city firm.

So, I decided I just had to go in my shorts and took the present Caroline had given me hoping it would make up for things. When I got there, the son told me that his elderly father had unfortunately left his hearing aids at home, and would I possibly mind joining him for lunch the next day at his favourite restaurant so that he could meet and hear me? Of course not, I said – I'd be honoured. I was now even more worried about what I was going to wear. All my travelling clothes were far too hot for the climate (it had been October in the UK and yet was summer over here), so again I had to just turn up in my shorts and tee-shirt – to one of the best restaurants in the capital. Edward didn't seem to mind a bit, although I did doubt that his hearing aids were working as he seemed to hear little I said. Given he didn't speak much English I ended up spending most of our lunch showing him photographs of our trip and listening to his Armenian stories.

Towards the end of the meal he put his napkin down, sat back in his chair and said: 'So, Jayne, tell me, how I can help? What would you like me to do?' I'm embarrassed to say I hadn't once thought about the fact he might want to donate to us. We hadn't set up the charity at this point, and I had no idea of the projects that Caroline had in mind. But here was a major opportunity.

All I could think to say was: 'Well, it was quite cold in the children's hospital, I believe their heating has broken and it is winter.' 'Perfect,' he replied, 'How much do you want?' I said I really didn't have any idea, but that I would get back to him straight away about it. He smiled and said he'd happily pledge a certain amount, which he wrote down, but which isn't for me to share here.

That was my first official fundraising ask, and it had worked. I was ecstatic and stunned.

It was a lesson I'd take into the future when I ended up directing fundraising for Oxfam, Tony Blair, and the Worldwide Association of Girl Guides and Girl Scouts. If you motivate donors with stories of real people, and earn their trust by being authentic, then they will ask *you* how they can help.

It's exactly the same with evangelism – share stories, be authentic, and they'll come and ask you about your faith.

———•———

The stories from my trip to Argentina could fill a book. I loved publicly ministering to people and witnessing the Holy Spirit powerfully at work. I visited various prisons and mental hospitals and learnt about the work being done by an army of hidden saints, who had given their lives to serving the poor. These were truly extraordinary people. However, the person who impacted my life the most while I was out there was an ex-soldier called Ruben, who had fought in the Falklands war.

Ruben had been asking me, through an interpreter, to go and see his work with the homeless and prostitutes from the moment I arrived. However, because of the language barrier it was difficult to arrange. I wanted to go, but I was also conscious that he seemed a little wary of me – I was English after all. He also seemed quite depressed. I mentioned this to the head of the YWAM base, and she explained that Ruben was severely behind with his lodging payments as he had no one supporting his work. They all believed God would intervene, but Ruben was understandably getting quite despondent and questioning whether this was truly where he was meant to be.

I made a point of prioritising joining him the next day, interpreter or no interpreter.

I'm so glad I did.

At the last moment one of the girls offered to come and

translate, which was a major blessing. He explained that Thursdays were the day that he held an indoor football match for all the street kids. I was a bit perplexed as to how this could possibly help them but decided to 'go with it'.

Like most Latin American countries (and European ones too) football was the national sport. What was news to me though was the fact that several of the bars in town had indoor football pitches attached to them. Ruben had approached one of them and explained his vision of helping the street kids get to know and trust each other. Most came from abusive backgrounds, and therefore found it incredibly hard to trust anyone, let alone form friendships. This meant that they were very vulnerable on the streets and had no one looking out for them. By bringing them together once a week, friendships were forming – and importantly, they were also able to have a weekly shower. I thought it was inspired and told him so. I asked him how I could help, and he suggested I brought some drinks and biscuits along for them to have some supper afterwards.

Later that evening the three of us were sat in McDonalds reflecting on the day's events. I had been deeply touched by what I had seen, and the love and respect these twenty young men – some just teenagers – had for him. I asked him what had motivated him to get involved with this work and he explained that he too had lived on the streets. Like many soldiers returning from the war he had found himself homeless and without a job. He had lost many of his friends in the Falklands and had become very bitter and angry with the government and most definitely with the English, who he still believed were the cause of the problem. I could see I was the last person he really wanted to be sharing all this with, and to be honest I really didn't know what to say or do.

So, I offered to buy him supper and just sat, listened, and cried – with him and for him. He too had lived alone on the streets, unsure of who to trust and yet scared to go to sleep because of what might happen to him if he did. He had had to beg, but instead of spending the money to get food and shelter, he had saved it up to buy a suit and rent a hotel room for a day. I was surprised by this and raised my eyebrows. 'Oh no, Jayne, it's not what you think,' he laughed, 'I needed to have a wash and a shave, I mean a real wash to get the street off me, so I could go and find a proper job.' It was this he was teaching his kids to do – showing them a way out of their mess. It was inspiring.

The next day I went with him, without an interpreter, to hand out sandwiches to the prostitutes in the main square. They all knew him and were standing waiting for him when we finally arrived – after having spent the morning making up dozens of baguettes. Over lunch he chatted to them all, one by one. All I could do was hand out the food with as big a smile as I could. For most, he was the only real and safe contact they had with any man – one who genuinely cared about them and looked out for them. Suddenly he looked around the group, and then spoke to one of the girls. Evidently one was missing – where was she? Was she all right? None of the girls had seen her either and they promised to look out for her. I could see Ruben was worried, but there was little he could do to help – save pray. I still don't know what happened to her.

I went back to the YWAM base and went straight to see the Director. I asked her how much Ruben owed, and told her I would pay it off in cash. It was a couple of years' worth of debt but given the currency difference a fraction of what it would have been in the UK. I too had little money, but I knew my chances of being able to raise it were far greater than his – and I had the remainder of my generous gift for starters. The only condition was that I didn't want him to know it was me – although, as the Director said, he was probably going to guess!

He came bounding up to me the next day, gave me a huge hug and said: '*La dama inglesa*[3]!' Yes, I thought, I bet the last

[3] The English Lady!

person you expected to help you would be an English woman, especially given everything you've been through. God definitely has a sense of humour – or is it healing?

He called over the girl who had interpreted for us on our first day and she explained that he wanted, by way of thanks, to show me around his city as he knew I had yet to do any sightseeing. I said I'd love that. The only snag was that our bilingual friend was sadly unable to join us as she had a church commitment. I smiled and said I was sure we'd get by, which we somehow did. He spoke Spanish, I English, with lots of accompanying hand signals and facial expressions.

We had the most amazing day. We visited the Presidential palace on the Plaza de Mayo, then La Boca – with the famous painted houses and we even tried our hand (or is it feet) at the Tango. We talked for hours – although I think we only understood about half of what each other said. I could see his heart, he mine. We both loved Jesus, and both knew the key was to JUST LOVE.

I began to wonder if I had just met my husband. I thought it an unusual match, but then that was God all over. He was an attractive man, a bit of a rough diamond perhaps, but the thing that drew me to him was not that but rather his heart for God. The problem was the distance between us – not an easy commute, and we were so obviously called to serve in each of our respective countries.

Later the next week I was able to link him with a local pastor I had met. He too went to visit Ruben's work, and was bowled over by it. His church got behind it, and the next thing I knew was that they had raised funds for him to buy a minibus, so he could help look after more people.

The last I heard he was still working there, and his ministry had grown exponentially. Praise God!

———◆———

Back in the UK, I was about to enter my last year on Council. I was busy setting up the charities for both Andrew and Caroline, and I also found myself being heavily involved with various projects behind the scenes in Parliament. Foremost of these was the Manchester Group, led by the Bishop of Manchester, which I'd set up to co-ordinate a religious response to the Broadcasting Bill and its implications.

There were other parliamentary initiatives led by a range of para-church groups, and many with connections to Prayer for Parliament. This was an evangelical group that met to pray every so often in the Undercroft, a gilded chapel directly under the Great Hall in the Houses of Parliament.

I had been given the use of some office space on Buckingham Palace Road, which belonged to the Duke of Westminster. Most of these were rented out at peppercorn rates to charities – although the competition was fierce. A friend had let me share his rooms so that I could base both Caroline's and Andrew's work together, while I tried to secure some rooms for the longer term.

This friend, Anthony, worked as a mentor with many of the Christian MPs in Parliament, and had helped link me with the National Prayer Breakfast crowd in Washington DC, which was led by Doug Coe. These Americans seemed to me a little like the Christian equivalent of the Mafia, with a network of senior evangelicals across most states – virtually all Republicans. They owned a very impressive building called The Cedars on the banks of the Potomac in Virginia, just across from Washington DC. It had originally been owned by Howard Hughes and was modelled on the White House. Visiting Christian dignitaries and diplomats would be invited there to stay when they were in Washington DC, to ensure that they had a Christian 'home from home'.

Caroline and I were able to stay there once, which was highly unusual as they were not that used to female guests. I remember the grand staircase and the lush furniture – an

It's Raining Men!

American version of a palace. Frankly, it was far nicer than the West Wing, which we were about to visit for lunch.

Anthony was a great support and encourager to me, right from the first day I was interviewed for Council, when he had taken me to lunch in the Houses of Parliament. Nearly thirty years my senior, he too had an incredible heart for serving God at any cost – and had done so for many years, working behind the scenes with great humility and grace. It was from him I learnt what it is to be hidden, and how I needed to accept the importance of that in my work.

He too lived by faith, and I took inspiration from that. I remember once reflecting in a Council meeting when we were reviewing clergy stipend levels, that it would be interesting to know how many clergy believed in their calling enough to trust God if their stipend was removed. There was quite an outcry around the table at this suggestion, and one of the bishop's turned to me and said: 'But, Jayne, you don't understand. Please remember most have families and other commitments.'

'Don't you think God knows that?' I replied, a little brusquely. 'I mean, He knows our situation better than we do.' I decided it was best not to raise the question again – well, not until I wrote a book.

I really liked Anthony, and particularly loved his passion for God and his spiritual maturity. I began to wonder if we too might be destined for each other – despite the obvious age gap, and the fact he was only just recently widowed. The important thing, I reflected, was that I was meeting men who I felt drawn towards – primarily because of our deep spiritual connection, and the fact we therefore understood each other. I therefore believed I was healed, and that I was on a new path.

———•———

Things had been brought home to me about the need for the

Church to deal urgently with the issue of sexuality earlier that summer, when Peter Tatchell and a small group of demonstrators had disrupted the York Synod. It was a tense stand-off, with no one knowing quite what to do. Peter was standing on the stage surrounded by a group of LGBT Christians, holding placards and shouting various things at the Archbishops. They had no microphones, so all I could hear was him shouting 'Your Grace! Your Grace!'.

Being seated near one of the floor microphones, I stood up and found myself saying: 'Peter, you say "Your Grace, Your Grace", but where is the Grace in all this? Can I suggest that we all *say* the Grace, and then we go outside and discuss things together there?' I then started reciting the Grace, and to my relief others joined in. Once we were finished, and the demonstration had left the stage, I went out to meet them – hoping others would join me there too. No one did – except the media, who were out in force. 'What are you going to say, Jayne?' a reporter asked as I made towards the group. 'I'm not going to say anything,' I replied, 'I'm going to go and listen!'

The group were understandably angry and upset. Many had placards with pictures of friends who I suspected had sadly committed suicide. They told me how frustrated they were with the Church – and I said I understood. But, I told them, demonstrating like this was not the way to get people to hear them. 'We've tried talking to them,' one young man said, who I recognised as having been on Synod a few years earlier, 'but they just don't want to listen.' He was right of course – the Church didn't want to listen. It was steeped in discussions around whether women could be in the episcopate and hadn't the energy or the space to cope with other issues of injustice.

However, the next 2004 February Synod we did make a start by debating *Issues in Human Sexuality*. I felt I ought to put in to speak given my testimony, but I had no idea what I should say. After a fair bit of prayer, I decided to write a speech that tried to highlight the anguish of those having to deal with

It's Raining Men!

the conflict between their faith and their sexuality. I sat and wrote it in the form of a suicide note. It was not one I had ever prepared, but it certainly summed up the heart-ache and pain that I had felt, and which had nearly taken me over the edge. It started as follows:

'Where are You, God? I cannot see anything. It's too dark. It's too painful. I cannot feel anything. I lost that ability a long time ago. How can You abandon me here, alone in this no man's land of nothingness? I cannot go back. What good could it do if I could, anyway? It's far too complex a path to retrace. I haven't the strength or the desire to move on. Tomorrow will only be full of the same confusion and screaming pain. Living in the present without hope or meaning is unbearable, and I so wish that I could put an end to it all. But that is not an option either, is it? You wouldn't approve of my taking that easy way out, would You?

So why leave me here? Why can You not do something? Why can I not feel You? Why have You let go of my hand? I've talked to my doctors and my psychiatrists. They tell me it is simple: I should change my religion. They just do not understand, and why should they? I wish I could talk to someone, anyone, who can help put an end to this short-circuiting in my brain – this tormenting that keeps going round and round in circles, driving me quite literally mad. I know in my head that You are the God of love. You created me to love – but how? If the only thing that I long and pray for is the one thing that I am forbidden, can this be true? I do not understand. You seem to be punishing me and I am trapped in this hell of deep despair: longing to find a way out of this prison cell. So how can I live? Just how do You expect me to go on?'[4]

4 General Synod Report on Proceedings – Wednesday 11th February 2004 (p. 261)

Just Love

The problem was, was I to give this speech in the 'first person' or the 'third person'? I had absolutely no idea. I knew which would be the more powerful, and which would cause the greatest stir – but was I ready for that? I decided the best thing was to go and speak to a friend, Steve Jenkins, who was the senior press officer in the Church of England's Communications Unit.

On the morning of the debate, with both versions of the speech in hand, I asked to see him. I gave him the excerpt set out above to read, and then explained my dilemma – did I own this as my own suicide note or not? He was in effect the first person I told within the central Church, save Bishop Michael, and bless him he didn't bat an eyelid. What he was immediately clear about though was how the media would react to my speech – particularly the tabloids, who would have a feeding frenzy.

'Jayne, if you say this is your own note then please know that if you have any skeletons in your cupboard they will come out. I'm not going to advise you either way, but you need to know they'll go through your past with a toothcomb. They'll contact your family too – do your parents know?'

I decided the best policy was to leave it all in the hands of Mr God – maybe I wouldn't get called to speak anyway. So, like others, I stood to indicate I wanted to speak throughout the debate. I began to believe I was going to be let off the hook – it didn't look like I was going to be called after all. The Chairman indicated that there would be one last speech before moving to the amendments, and I breathed a sigh of relief. I then heard my name being called out. I stood and realised that those near me could see I was shaking. In fact, I was shaking so much it was difficult to read my speech.

Nerves, I think most thought – although those who knew me well knew I was rarely that nervous when speaking.

I started the speech as above, knowing it was quite different to the other speeches and continued:

It's Raining Men!

'This is one of the many personal testimonies, written by someone who had a breakdown (I did give it in the Third Person) over the tension between their faith and their confused sexual identity.

I have prayed with many such people and seen them bravely walk down that long and difficult path of emotional and spiritual healing, under the transforming power of the Holy Spirit. Many, but not all, find that their natural desires change and that they are able to move on, into a lifelong heterosexual relationship. The key to coming out of their prison? For many, it is the step of getting real about how they feel, the traumas they have been through, and the anger they felt, often towards God Himself. However, all those whom I have met have one thing in common. They found that their churches were the last place that they felt they could discuss their confusion and pain. For many, this was because they feared being boxed or labelled. Even a mere admission that they were confused about their sexual identity ran the risk of being labelled as 'unsound' or 'a liability'; but where could they turn to for help? Where would you turn if you were faced with the same confusion and pain?

I know that many of us pride ourselves that our churches are open, loving, accepting places, but are they really? Are they understanding? Are they safe? Much public criticism has been made of the Church as being homophobic. The question is, are we? I believe that, to answer this, we first need to answer the question, each of us, individually. But how do we know? I would ask you, if the opening paragraph had been written by the person sitting next to you, would that change your view of them? Would you want to draw back? Would you see them as somehow different to the person that you knew before? If you find that the answer is yes, then I would suggest that you are indeed homophobic.'

Just Love

Who'd have guessed that thirteen years later I would be leading my own Private Members Motion debate in Synod to get the Church to condemn the very Conversion Therapy that I had advocated in this speech. The motion was overwhelmingly endorsed (only one bishop voted against it), and it led to the Synod calling on the government for it to be banned.

CHAPTER TEN

Junta in the Jungle

December 2004

I decided to leave the Archbishops' Council with a bit of a bang – after all, I thought, it was my final chance to air my views, and I might as well make the most of it.

I had been put down to lead the opening worship of my last meeting, which was to be held in the Library at Lambeth Palace – around the specially commissioned Archbishops' Council's table.

I had just arrived back from an exhilarating yet harrowing trip to South East Asia where we had smuggled aid into Myanmar, and distributed funds to refugees in the Thai-Burmese borderlands. It had been a trip of many answered prayers, not least when we had ventured into Myanmar and heard that the military Junta were active in the area, making us quickly change our route.

We were met in the makeshift refugee village of rickety wooden shacks built on stilts by Rainbow – a young man with a broad smile and a huge heart. He had taken in many of the orphans in the area and was trying to teach them so that they had a basic education. He explained that no aid had been getting through and that they were down to just a few sacks of rice. The next delivery was not due for another three months, and they had no money to buy any rice themselves.

That morning I and the two trustees I was travelling with had prayed about how much cash we should take with us that day. I was travelling with a significant sum so that we could give it out to the various projects we were visiting, but the challenge was always to know how much to give to each project as we had no idea of the need that we might meet around the corner. We had all agreed a specific – very generous – sum, which I had counted out and put in a white envelope.

We proceeded to the one large communal space in the village, where we sat on the floor with Rainbow and the village elder. They explained how the Junta were stepping up activities but that for the present they were safe – unlike the refugees we had met at a camp on the border a few days before. Sadly, many there had lost limbs by stepping on landmines while trying to escape.

Feeling for the envelope in my bag, I said we had a gift for them. We were sorry it couldn't be more, but that we hoped it would go some way to helping them. Rainbow beamed, and I remember thinking how on earth did he stay so positive in such difficult circumstances?

'Thank you, lady,' he said, 'God told me you come today. I saw you in night in dream – white English lady. You have white envelope for us. It has money to buy rice for three months.'

I looked at my colleagues amazed, got out the white (not the usual brown) envelope and passed it over. Rainbow thanked us, and I asked him how much it would cost to buy rice for the village for three months? He said the exact amount we had agreed to that morning. I was speechless.

The more sobering part of the trip though was visiting the traumatised children in the orphanages Caroline had helped set up in the Thai-Burmese borderlands. We'd been asked to bring paper and colouring pens along with the usual tins of biscuits so that the children could draw their memories of home as a form of art therapy. Nothing could have prepared me for the results. Homes on fire, men in helicopters shooting people, blood sacks[1]

[1] A gruesome practice of draining someone's blood into a sack and pinning it on a washing line as a warning to others

hanging on washing lines, paddy fields bombed.

Many readers may have seen the terrible reports of displaced Rohingya Muslims in the news. The awful truth is that this sort of ethnic cleansing, which Caroline and others are convinced is genocide, had been going on for years amongst most of the minority groups in Myanmar. We had visited representatives from many communities, such as the Mon, the Shan, the Karen and the Karenni – all had terrible stories to tell. Paddy fields mined, villages raised, cooking pots shot right through – which is a small but highly strategic act. How do you best ensure the elimination of a people? By taking away their ability to cook and therefore eat – a sure sign of genocidal intent.

———————

It was these children's drawings I took with me to my last Archbishops' Council meeting. I put one in each of twenty-five large brown envelopes marked 'Do Not Open Until Told to Do So' and placed them in every place setting around the table. I started the worship by explaining that I had just returned from Myanmar, and that I had been working with orphaned children there, who had drawn their memories of home. I suggested we kept these children at the front of our minds not just during the worship but also during our meeting as we talked about financial matters. I then invited people to open their envelopes – the shock was palpable; the point was made. We were so rich – we had peace, safety, security, food, a home ….

Over lunch, Archbishop Rowan thanked me publicly. It had been meant to be a double farewell for both Archbishop David and myself, but sadly Archbishop David was ill. I wasn't too sure what Archbishop Rowan was going to say, but was very touched and grateful when he said:

'I've been trying to think how best to sum up Jayne's unique role amongst us on Council. I'm not sure if any of you have watched *Indiana Jones and the Last Crusade* (laughter), but for those who haven't it happens to be about the search for the Holy Grail. The only way Indiana Jones is finally able to determine which is the authentic grail, is by reflecting on who it is *actually there to serve*. I believe Jayne has constantly brought us back to the question, "Who are we here to serve?"'

I had prepared a one-page hand out summarising my parting thoughts for Council about some of the challenges that I believed lay ahead, which I asked permission to distribute at the end of the meeting. It was a rather hard-hitting piece, which ended up causing quite a stir – especially given it was covered in *The Times* the next day. In fact, it made for an interesting tube journey home for me later that night, as I couldn't help noticing my picture on the open page of the newspaper of the man sitting next to me. I asked if there was any way he'd mind me having a read and looking at the picture and then back at me, he grinned and said: 'Here, love, I think you need this far more than me!'

That was my last day on Council.

―――――•♦•―――――

The next two years were a complete rollercoaster, not least because of the significant changes I would make both at home and on the job front.

Around Easter 2005 I met the Revd David MacInnes, who had come to lead our parish away-day. By now I was worshipping at St Simon's, Rockley Road – the church situated just a few doors up from my flat, which was led by a friend, the Revd Sonya Arnold. David was very worried about my workload and convinced me that I really needed to choose between the two charities I was running.

This was so difficult. Both were doing the most incredible work. I had just come back from Moscow, where I had been visiting our orphanage there and trying to meet with potential funders from my Kimberly-Clark days. As usual on these trips

Junta in the Jungle

I had met some of the most inspirational people – this time it was an extraordinary American lady from Saddleback Church in California, which was led by Rick Warren. She was married to a quadriplegic, and together over the years they had adopted dozens of disabled children from around the world. Because of her husband's situation they had designed their house to cater for a range of mobility needs. In fact, this wonderful lady felt called to go around the world looking for children that nobody else 'wanted'. She was particularly concerned about the plight of Russian children, given rumours that they could often go missing.

I arrived at the orphanage the day before she did, and so I'd had the chance to meet twelve-year-old Michael, who was one of the two boys she was coming to 'take home'. Michael was a delight; sadly, due to being dropped as a baby, he had no use of his right arm and walked with a very pronounced limp. When I met him in the evening he was so excited. He didn't speak any English but that didn't deter him – he just chattered away to me in Russian explaining how happy he was that he was finally going to have a mummy. The next morning at breakfast, however, he was completely different and very subdued. I asked him, through our interpreter, what the matter was. The interpreter and Michael had a long chat, and eventually she turned to me and said: 'He's scared she won't want him. He's petrified she'll take one look at him and leave him here.'

My heart broke. This poor boy had been awake all the night crying, and he looked dreadful.

We both assured him as best we could that she would definitely want him and love him, and that's why she was flying all the way over from the United States to be able to take him home. He wasn't convinced. I went with the Orphanage Director to the airport to meet her and explained in the car on the drive back what he had said. 'Oh, that's completely normal, Jayne,' she said. 'Don't worry, they all feel that – but you wait, I've got a CD player for him in my bag and I'm going to tell him he'll be able to learn to drive when he's old enough.' I looked quizzically at her, and she read my thoughts. She went on to explain that she and her husband had created a business that adapted homes and cars for people with mobility needs, so all their children could benefit.

What a woman! A true saint in action – but sadly with little support from her church.

I was convinced I should choose to work with Caroline, but within five minutes of making that decision Mr God had made it abundantly clear that I should instead focus on Andrew's ground-breaking work. Although his original focus had been to work with Lord Carey to oversee the religious track of the Peace Process in the Middle East, he was now spending significant amounts of his time helping the American administration in their reconstruction efforts in Iraq.

Fortunately, both charities seemed to understand my dilemma. After finishing my work with Caroline, I set about focusing full time on creating some structure for the new Foundation for Reconciliation and Relief, which we had just successfully launched in the House of Lords.

However, I was beginning to feel uneasy in my spirit. I sensed things were all in flux – and although I couldn't quite put my finger on it, I knew that some type of 'season change' was happening.

The words I kept hearing was that I was 'to do an Abraham', whatever that meant. I began to feel restless and realised that I no longer felt as at home in London as I had done. I missed water and the countryside – trees, fields and rolling hills. There was none of that in Shepherd's Bush.

I also felt that I was not the right person to take the Foundation forward into its next phase. My skills were more about galvanising people to start new initiatives, not managing the day to day. Also, it wasn't that easy being a woman in such a male-dominated Muslim world. Iraq was fast becoming our fulltime focus, and it was impossible for me to travel out there given the war.

By the summer of 2005 I decided to do what I believed Mr God had been telling me to do. I knew it would be controversial, but then I was never one for doing things by the book.

I put my house on the market and gave my notice to all the Boards and Councils on which I served – including those at Trinity Theological College, and the Church of England Newspaper, which were both chaired by my close friend and ex-Council colleague, Bishop Michael Nazir-Ali. I also gave the Foundation notice of my resignation, so that they could set about looking for someone else.

As it happened, I had recently spoken at Lee Abbey in Devon and had made some good friends there – including Emma Ineson and Chris Edmondson. Chris suggested I went to join them for a bit while I tried to work out what my next 'chapter' looked like – which at the time seemed a completely blank page. After going back to Guernsey to look after my mother, who had just had major surgery, I booked myself into Tinkerbell – a tiny studio in the grounds of Lee Abbey. It was in the middle of the woods overlooking the sea – an oasis of calm. However, I soon realised six weeks was going to be a long time of waiting and praying. Chris called me their 'resident hermit', but in truth I found the solitude challenging – and the woods quite frightening, especially at night.

I walked, I read, I walked some more. I learnt to make smoothies out of freshly picked berries and helped a bit with things at the Abbey, notably with a royal visit to mark their sixtieth anniversary.

The only problem was, I had absolutely no sense at all as to what was coming next. It was infuriating. All those years when I felt I had heard God so clearly when I least expected it, and now – when I was ready, waiting, and in need of direction – nothing. That was, apart from an overwhelming desire to read about international relations and the abuse of power.

My time was running out, and I was beginning to panic.

I now had a buyer for my flat, and the completion date was set for late January 2006.

My only 'back-up' plan was with my old friend Veronica – who had been Archbishop George's Private Secretary, and an old prayer partner. She had moved to Oxford a few years earlier and had held a party where we were able to reconnect – just after I got back from Lee Abbey. She asked what I was up to and I explained I was in the process of selling up and putting everything into storage as I felt I was being called to 'do an Abraham' and go somewhere new. Knowing me of old, and with the extraordinary gift of hospitality that she has always shown, Veronica said: 'Well, Jayne, if you ever need a place to stay, you're always very welcome to my spare room in Oxford.'

Oxford? Now there was a thought. I had always been drawn to Oxford – right from my school days when I had wanted to try and buck our school trend and apply there instead of Cambridge. It was ideally placed close to London, and within an hour's drive of both Bristol and Southampton airports in case I needed to get home to Guernsey. Most importantly it had a large evangelical church led by two wonderful people, Charlie and Anita Cleverly, who had been very supportive of me when I spoke out in a New Wine Leader's Meeting. I had challenged them all to consider just how open they really were about talking honestly about sexuality issues with each other, and whether we were truly loving. Charlie had come to talk to me afterwards and had then supported me in prayer.

So, after finally selling my house I moved to Oxford in March 2006 with a view of getting actively involved with life at St Aldates and seeing what new opportunities arose.

Veronica was amazing and welcomed me warmly into her home. The first night, after cooking me supper, she asked me whether I had any sense of what the future held. I explained that I had sadly no idea but that I had a strange peace about it all, and that I believed all would be revealed at the right time. I was where I believed I was meant to be, and that's what really mattered.

I did want to reassure her though that I wasn't planning on staying with her indefinitely – in fact, I had already started to look at houses in the area. I added that I had a growing desire to research international power structures and was keen to see if or how they were reflected in the Bible. I then explained that the role of religion in international relations also fascinated me, which was quite a new concept at the time. From my own experience of conflict areas where tensions between religions played a key factor, I realised that solutions were never going to be found until the West took the role of religion seriously. They needed to see it as part of the solution, not just the problem. However, most governments were averse to this and I believed that only research from the top academic institutions was going to change the situation. I asked her whether she knew how I might try to get a University library card so that I could continue my research?

'Have you thought of applying to do a formal post-graduate degree?' Veronica said, which suddenly resonated with me. 'I happen to know they've just brought out a new MA in Global Governance.'

Bingo! That was it! It was as if the floodgates of my mind had opened. Of course, I could do some formal research into the global power bases such as the UN and NATO and look at how they were formally constituted. Were they truly as bad and unaccountable as my American friends feared?

I went to speak to the University the very next day and learnt that unfortunately the MA course was already full. However, they suggested that I might want to consider applying for the Foreign Service Programme, which was a post-graduate course they ran in International Diplomacy.

'Isn't that just for diplomats, and in particular overseas diplomats?' I asked.

Well yes, I was told, but my time working with Andrew

and Caroline had given me a significant amount of on the ground experience, and they were keen to have a UK student. What's more, they were very positive about me wanting to look at the religious dimension within international relations. Indeed, as we were to meet senior diplomats when we visited the UN, NATO, the EU and the European Court of Human Rights, I could ask them myself about any concerns I had.

The only slight snag was the cost – I was to be charged overseas rates, which were nearly three times that of UK student rates. I needed to make sure that this was definitely the 'right next step', but at least with the capital from my house sale I had the means to do it should I want to.

I decided to apply and see whether I was offered a place. I recognised it was very late in the academic year to be applying, and that I didn't meet their typical criteria. If this unusual door opened, then I would walk through it – as it made sense of my increasing desire to study international relations and international power politics, as well as my feeling so drawn to Oxford.

At the same time, I decided to 'cover my options' by applying to some consultancy firms. I was well qualified for this given my past consultancy roles and senior management experience, especially managing various large international brands. However, my first rejection letter was very sobering and helped me to realise the dilemma that my years of 'living by faith' had created. The Director of a well-known branding consultancy had written to me personally to explain that while I had excellent credentials and a significant amount of relevant experience, it was quite clear from my recent work with the Archbishops' Council and the various charities that I had recently set up and managed, that I was a woman who 'followed her heart'. Their concern was that I was not that committed to working in business, and they (correctly) guessed that I was only needing a stop-gap job until the 'next door' opened. They wanted and needed people to whom a job with their firm was the pinnacle of their career, and they realised that that would just not be the case for me.

It was a very honest letter, and I was extremely grateful to the Director for writing it as it brought things into sharp focus. It was the start of me understanding just how difficult it would be for me to get a 'proper' job in the 'real world'. I was far too qualified for most 'middle management' roles, especially as few wanted someone who would be perceived as a threat to their colleagues. At the same time, I was not seen as a 'sound enough choice' for senior management roles, given my proven tendency to 'follow my heart'. My other option was to look at the Christian NGO sector, which was primarily made up of evangelical charities, but as I was soon to realise – these too would close their doors when I finally embraced my God-given sexuality.

Interestingly, the other idea that kept nagging away at the back of my mind was whether I should have heeded all the calls from those around me on Council to consider ordination. I had strongly resisted this while on Council, as I truly believed that my calling was to be a senior *lay* leader. However, I began to wonder whether that season might have changed. The last thing I wanted was for my past thinking to get in the way, and so I decided the best thing to do was to go and talk it through with someone who knew me well, and who was a senior member of the House of Bishops.

As we sat in his office, I explained that I knew that I had a call on my life, but that up till now I had felt specifically that I was *not* to be ordained. I did not have a sense of being drawn to parish ministry, but I did feel very drawn to ministering to the international diplomatic community – and that I had in fact just been accepted on a programme at Oxford University, which would see me thrown right into the heart of this world. I therefore wondered if it might be possible to consider a 'fresh expression' of becoming a chaplain to the diplomatic world, with a specific role of encouraging a deeper understanding of the role of religion within the international institutions.

I remember my friend standing by the fireplace and staring into it as he contemplated what to say. After a long pause, he said – still looking into the fire – 'Jayne, I think God has shown that He can use you powerfully without you having to get ordained, and my fear is that if we did ordain you we would stop you from being all that you have been called to be. I don't think you need to get ordained to follow your calling.' I felt so relieved – but at least I had asked the question.

That door too was shut – although I would continue to press on it every so often, just to make sure.

God must have other plans I thought.

———•———

The one thing I was clear about was the fact that I needed to find a new home.

I needed 'rooting' somewhere, and I was convinced that this was meant to be somewhere near Oxford. I had started looking earlier in the New Year, before I had even sold my house, as I was keen to see the sort of thing that might be available to me within my price bracket.

The key picture I had in mind was of a house with a view, where I could sit and write a book (like this one). Originally, I had pictured a view over rolling hills, but I soon began to realise that being out in the countryside would be quite isolating – especially given I was living alone. I therefore decided to look nearer to Oxford and shelved 'my dream' of a writer's den.

The very first place I saw was a beautiful Grade II listed cottage in Littlemore, in south Oxford. According to the listing it was over 600 years old and had many period features. It had two large double bedrooms, one with built-in wardrobes and a dressing area, and a small downstairs study. With off street parking and a small but secluded walled garden – including a pond and a south facing patio, it seemed idyllic. What was even more exciting was that it had a large window box that overlooked the walled garden and pond, in which I could just fit my writing desk!

The only problem of course was the price – it was well over my budget and took me into a stamp duty range that I couldn't afford. In addition, I had concerns about the surrounding area. I had noticed large metal gates that enclosed the property next door, and barbed wire around the property across the road. Given I had been the first person to see it I assumed that despite these concerns it would probably be gone within the week – it was such a 'bijoux' treasure of a house.

After being formally accepted onto the course in April, I started to look again at houses, and went to see a property in nearby Cumnor. On recognising my unusual surname, the estate agent tentatively asked me: 'Weren't you the lady who was interested in our little cottage in Littlemore? Can I ask why you decided not to go for it? It seemed to suit you perfectly.'

'You can't seriously be telling me it's still available?' I replied, somewhat surprised. 'Well, yes,' the agent admitted. 'It's quite a mystery to us – it's one of the nicest properties we've had for ages, and yet hardly anyone is viewing it … which is why I wanted to ask what had put you off?'

I explained my concerns, especially about the gates and the barbed wire, and the estate agent laughed. 'Well the first is because the house next door was a Post Office and the gates were for that, and the second is because there was a research lab there where there was highly confidential work going on,' she said. 'Would you like to see it again? The sellers are really keen to sell as they've a property they're desperate to buy – I think you may find they'd be quite flexible with the price!'

So, I went around that evening with Veronica, and we both agreed it was utterly perfect. Neither of us could understand why I had even hesitated, apart from, of course, the price – which the owners were now willing to move on. What was more, I suddenly learnt I had some endowment funds that I could release, which just happened to cover the shortfall – and the additional stamp duty.

As always, there were snags. It failed the structural surveys due to an upstairs wall that was significantly out of line – but a Structural Engineer's report that was duly provided by the sellers seemed to satisfy that problem. In addition, various opinions from architects and builder friends convinced me this was a good investment. The location was excellent, and the listing was a bonus – there were few old properties like this around, and it would always keep its value.

Somehow, despite being a student and not having had a 'proper job' for several years, I was able to get a mortgage. So, in late August I exchanged contracts, and in early September 2006 I completed on the purchase.

For a fair bit of these intervening months I had been housesitting for the Cleverlys, as they had been travelling and were keen to have someone look after their house. After they returned they had kindly suggested I could stay on as my house purchase was imminent (or so it kept seeming). This meant we became close friends, and I was made to feel part of their family. In fact, Anita, who was then Head of the Lydia Prayer Movement, and I decided to become prayer partners.

The dream house finally bought, I moved in two weeks before my Oxford University course started.

CHAPTER ELEVEN

Back to School

September 2006

First day of school – I wonder if you remember yours?

That feeling of wondering whether the other kids will be nice? Whether they'll like you? Whether you'll like them? Everyone desperately keen to impress – everyone desperately keen to 'fit in'.

When I was at Procter & Gamble I was involved in making the Lenor 'First Day at School' advert, which was the company's first attempt at trying to sell something by pulling on consumers' heart strings. The advert was quite simple really – a little boy is taken to his first day of school by his mummy, who waves goodbye to him at the school gates. It's his first foray into life without her. After the initial excitement he starts to miss her. Snuggling into his school jumper, which has been freshly washed, he smells the familiar smell that reminds him of her and bounces back to life.

There was a large part of me that really wanted a metaphorical jumper to snuggle into that first day at Oxford. I felt so completely out of sorts – back in a classroom after so many years in the 'real' world, treated like a teenager by the porters (who weren't used to having mature students around) and wondering where this was all going to lead to. I just wanted something that would remind me of the world I had come from – this all felt so utterly alien to me.

We were an unlikely bunch – drawn together from across the world and for differing reasons.

Some had been sent because they were the 'crème de la crème' of their diplomatic core, others because they were to be given an 'Oxford education' by their ruling families (to which they themselves were invariably related), others because their mission didn't know what to do with them and still others because it was viewed as a major reward for their loyalty of service. For most it demanded great sacrifice – a whole year away from their spouse and young families (as most of my colleagues were indeed young and at the start of their careers). For instance, the wife of our Chinese representative had a baby in his first term – their one and only child. He didn't see his daughter for the whole of her first year. One of our Japanese colleagues arrived speaking no English and was put on an intensive two-week course. Failure was not an option given his culture, and my heart went out to him as he struggled to learn a language while studying at one of the toughest universities in the world. I gave him all my notes and essays and tried to help as much as I could.

There were just over two dozen of us – from as diverse a group of countries as China, South Korea, Ghana, Japan, Jamaica, Algeria, Malta, Kosovo, Russia, Turkey and Romania. In fact, we had three Romanians – it was the first year their country had participated in the programme, and so we had a triple blessing. I do wonder what my life would have been like if there had only been two.

I'm not sure what it is about me and foreign women. Maybe it's their seductive accent? Maybe it's the intensity of the friendship, given one of us is in a strange country away from home? Maybe it's because I just happen to have been incredibly fortunate to have met some extremely attractive and intelligent women who wanted to become my friend, and who I loved spending time with?

I so wish I could remember how we first really got to know each other – Gabi and me. So much of the next two years was to become a blur as I struggled to cope with the waves of emotional and mental anguish, which even now I find painful to recall. There are things I know I have blocked – the body is very good at self-preservation when it needs to be.

The year was a whirlwind of lectures, supervisions, formal dinners with visiting speakers and trips abroad. It was a fascinating course – not least because of the access it gave to some of the most senior diplomats and civil servants of our generation. In fact, one of my lasting memories was being shown a scene from *Yes, Prime Minister* by one of our after-dinner speakers who – pointing at Sir Humphrey Appleby – laughingly said to us: 'That's me! It really was just like this, you know!'

Our first trip at the end of our first term was to Northern Ireland to meet those involved in brokering the Good Friday agreement – seen as one of the greatest diplomatic coups of our time. A friend had arranged for me to meet the Speaker of the House at Stormont for a private briefing and I had asked our Programme Director if Gabi could join me given the unique opportunity we had. Sadly, he said no for reasons that weren't particularly clear, which she (like I) was deeply frustrated about. But what was clear was that by the time of that particular trip she had become a dear and trusted friend, and someone whose company I sought out above all others.

However, it wasn't till our next overseas trip in March 2007 – to visit the UN and NATO in Geneva as well as the Council of Europe, the European Parliament and the European Court of Human Rights in Strasbourg – that I realised I had a 'problem'. A really quite serious problem.

I do remember recognising that quite distinctly.

Gabi and I were sat on the back row of the coach – the place I had always associated with adolescent teenagers. To be more precise, Gabi was stretched out across the back seats and I was sat on the floor next to her, so we could talk. I must admit it was rather uncomfortable – but I just loved being with her, and talking to her, and listening to her. If that meant a bit of discomfort well so be it. And then it hit me, what *was* I doing down there? This was not normal – sitting on the floor of a moving coach. I tried to push the thoughts that were coming through my mind away – they came like tennis balls from a service machine, and it took all my strength to hit them back.

Later that evening in our hotel, Gabi came around to my room – dressed in her pyjamas. She was always the night-owl and couldn't sleep. So, we sat on my bed and talked, just as friends do. We laughed about one of our colleagues who had had an eyebrow shaved off by his 'friends' in his sleep (which he was understandably livid about), and somehow the conversation came around to the point where Gabi offered to do my eyebrows for me. I was grateful, as it was something I always found difficult to do myself, and the next thing I knew I was laid back on my bed with this stunningly beautiful woman staring down at me, looking straight into my eyes as she focused on her work. The proximity, the closeness, the intimacy – it took every ounce of strength not to act on the urges that were suddenly raging unwittingly through my body.

I froze.

The feelings were back – in force. They were real and unavoidable.

There was only one word for it – desire. I suddenly knew and understood its meaning. It's not something you can ever be taught about – you might see it in films or read about it in books, but until you have experienced it first hand, you have no idea of its power. It is quite literally a force of nature. And no, I had not felt it like that before, well certainly not with men. Yes, I might have recognised in my head that certain guys were desirable, that they were good intellectual or spiritual matches for me, but I had not felt this level of physical attraction before. It was as if I had been hit by a bus – such an overwhelming feeling, which was totally beyond my control.

Unexpected and uninvited.

It was like two large magnets drawing two people together.

A force that we were powerless to stop. At least I presumed it was being mutually felt – how could it not be given its strength?

Confused, scared, and yet now fully alive, I tried to ask her about it the next day. I soon realised though that she hadn't felt a thing. Yet again I was in an unrequited situation of unwanted desire.

I came home from the trip – to my beautiful, God-given house – and sat down on the sofa and cried. Huge sobbing tears that welled up from the very centre of my being. Long silent screams that were lodged somewhere deep within my chest. I began to understand the phrase 'racked by grief', and as I wept I feared this sorrow would rip me apart. I think it's probably the only time I had ever cried for myself and by myself – something up till then I had found impossible to do.

I was an abomination – still. I had not been healed, despite all I had gone through. What really tore me apart was that I wanted to love and be loved more than anything, but what hope was there when the love I desired was such 'forbidden fruit'? I looked around the lounge and welled up again – I felt so utterly unworthy of this extraordinary house. Just looking at it reminded me of a God who had answered so many prayers, and yet for some reason had chosen not to answer the one prayer that mattered more than anything else to me. 'What had I done to bring this on myself?' I wondered. There had to be something – there must be a reason for such torment.

'I'm so sorry, Lord!' was all I could say, repeating it over and over again as I rocked back and forth.

I felt dirty, unworthy and so very alone. A 'woman of God' with a dark secret, that no one else I believed would ever understand. As strange as this may sound, I truly thought that I was the only evangelical Christian who had ever suffered being attracted to someone of the same sex.

I was back in hell, and this time I knew there was no way out.

After some thought, I decided my best strategy was to seek as much prayer as I could from people I trusted. Gabi had become my closest friend, and I wanted to be able to enjoy our friendship without all the complications of feeling attracted to her. Surely that was possible through prayer?

I talked to my Christian friends, and a consensus emerged that I was 'under spiritual attack'. Many within the various Prayer Movements who had been praying for me believed I was destined for 'great things', especially given how I had got onto my course in Oxford. They therefore felt that all this had been sent as a trial to knock me off-course. I needed to resist and 'stand firm', and the feelings would pass. As one dear friend lovingly wrote in a handwritten letter of concern for me:

> *'I really don't think Gabi is something; I think she represents something. What the Lord is about to do with you, where He is about to take you is, as you know, potentially so extraordinary that you have come under not just fire but cross fire ... so I guess that part of why I'm writing is to plead with you to desist from going somewhere it would be very difficult to return from ....'*

Many thought I just needed to 'claim my healing', and trust that God would not 'give me more than I could bear'. I became quite angry when anyone quoted this phrase at me – what did they know? The truth was that this was totally unbearable, and what's more God felt so absent. But what else could I do? I *had* to bear it, I had to just keep putting one foot in front of the other.

I was by now meeting frequently for prayer ministry sessions with Lin Button in London, whose ministry focused on emotional healing. After a time of me sharing and reflecting on what had been going on we would 'wait on the Holy Spirit', following which Lin would invariably have a picture for me, and we would then pray into that. Similarly, with my other prayer partners – Olave and Anita – we prayed for strength to stand against this attack. This would usually involve me repenting of my feelings and asking God to come and deliver me from this 'time of trial'.

Sometimes the prayer would work for a few weeks, months even, and I would euphorically believe that I had been healed. Then something would happen to make me realise I was still yearning for a love that was sinful and wrong, and I would find myself being overwhelmed once more.

Eventually, I felt I had no choice but to look for deeper causes. I had a friend who had been going through a significant amount of deliverance ministry, and he put me in touch with a couple in Oxford. They offered deliverance sessions at their home, and so I asked if they would see me.

I had no idea what I was going to be delivered of, but by this stage I was determined to try anything that might help. I just wanted to be rid of this turmoil, and to get back to 'normal' – whatever that was. My days with Caroline Cox and Andrew White seemed a life time away now.

I remember the first deliverance session clearly. I was sitting on the sofa praying, when suddenly I felt this weird sensation yet again of not being able to speak. It felt like a choking feeling, and they explained it was the evil spirits that were within me and which did not want to come out. They would call up all sorts of spirits – from lust to anger to fornication – and I would cough and splutter until they told me they had gone. Like others who had prayed for me before, they would ask me about all my sexual experiences – including the rape – and I would find myself sharing quite intimate details with people I barely knew. In hindsight, I think it incredible the trust we place in those who are perceived as having a gift for healing, and how vulnerable we can make ourselves.

There is a large part of me that would now call this type of ministry Spiritual Abuse.

You might be shocked by my decision to go through with all this – but please remember I believed I was doing it all out of obedience to Christ, and out of a desire to do 'whatever it takes' to get healed. I and those around me saw it as a test, where I was being asked to 'make myself nothing' – and so die to anything that would get in the way of my healing. This included my dignity and my fast diminishing sense of self-worth. The impact it would have on my spirit would be devastating.

I have no doubt that all those who prayed for me during this time did so out of an intense love for me, and a desire to see me healed. There was no hidden motive, although one could say that their own identity did rest in the fact they had a ministry – which I would give a donation to afterwards.

Thinking back, I realise I must have paid thousands of pounds to various people over the years – money I really didn't have, as I was 'living by faith' and had so little cash to spare. But a 'good workman is worthy of their hire' or so I was told. It just seemed to apply to everyone except me.

On moving to Oxford, I had thrown myself into life at St Aldates, where I sought to support Anita and Charlie as much as possible with their remarkable work leading one of the largest churches in Oxford. As such, I was particularly committed to being part of the Prayer Ministry team that frequently met for evening prayer sessions, and the Worship Group, where I played my violin.

The latter was something I dearly loved (and now sorely miss), and was something many agreed I had quite a unique gifting in. For some reason, as long as we were worshipping I could play 'completely by ear' without any music, and without any nerves. This meant I would hear a melody in my head and find that my fingers would somehow go straight to the notes. The key was never to think about it too much, but to just 'let it happen'. What I found most helpful though was to focus on someone who I could see had come forward for prayer and 'pray over them' with the music I was feeling led to play. I would try to 'tune in' to what I sensed they were feeling and reflect that in my music – from anger to sorrow, and from longing to joy.

I'd discovered this gifting quite by chance one evening back in the 1990s when I was at St Paul's Onslow Square. It was Christmas Eve, and John (our vicar) had asked if I could play for the midnight service as we were severely short on musicians. It was the first (and only) Christmas that my family had come to spend with me at my house, and I was loath to play as I wanted to sit with my mother for the service. But on arriving I realised that we were indeed very short in terms of a worship group – indeed it was just a cellist and myself. There were two sisters who were supposed to be joining us on strings – but they had not yet turned up.

The church was packed – which we should have been more prepared for given it was Midnight Mass in a large Anglican church in central Kensington. While we were waiting for the service to begin, John came up to me and whispered, 'Please play something, Jayne!' 'I can't!' I answered nervously, knowing how hard I found it to play on my own in public. 'Just play anything,' John begged. I could see we really did need some form of music, so I picked up my violin and started to play. 'That was beautiful,' one of the sisters said as they arrived to join me five or so minutes later. 'What was it?' 'I've no idea,' I replied – it's just where my fingers happened to fall.'

I had gone on to play in various worship bands, both at my London church and with Prayer for the Nations, which held large Prayer Meetings with international speakers in various central London venues. I became quite adapt at playing with loud electric bands – even with energetic drummers – and was fine so long as I had an earpiece that allowed me to hear myself play. By the time I had joined Martyn Layzell at St Aldates, I had quite a well-known style, and was completely at peace with playing solos on stage in front of thousands of people. This I saw as an undoubted answer to prayer, that utterly redeemed those traumatic days of playing solos in public when I was young.

———•———

Looking back at this time in Oxford I realise I was keen to do anything that I thought might ensure my healing. Worship was one such avenue, and so I sought to play as much as I could.

If I wasn't playing, I went forward for prayer ministry at the end of each service and made myself 'open' to whatever the Holy Spirit wanted to do. More often than not I felt it best not to say what was going on but found myself weeping uncontrollably in front of the altar – desperate for this burden to be lifted. Sadly, one of the legacies of all this is that I now find it very difficult to hear or participate in modern worship music without recalling these times of prayer ministry. It can act as a form of trigger, where I suddenly recall the grief, the pain, and the trauma of it all – so much so that I normally have to leave.

The diplomatic course seemed a whole different world away – although I did try once to mix them by inviting some colleagues to our Christmas Carol Service. It must have been quite a shock for those who agreed to come – not at all like the College Chapel Service that they were anticipating.

Interestingly, I had got to know the Dean and Chaplain of my College Chapel quite well and had become relatively involved with Magdalen Chapel as a result. I was therefore touched when I was asked if I would do one of the readings at the Magdalen Carols by Candle-light Service, to which I invited Charlie and Anita as a 'thank you' for all that they had done for me through the year.

The Fellow's Chaplain was a wonderful man called Angus

Ritchie, who was in the process of finishing his doctorate. I forget how we became such good friends, but by my second term we were meeting every week for tea to discuss our faith. I often wish we had followed through on our idea of writing a book to set out our different theological takes on things – Angus as an Anglo-Catholic and I as a charismatic evangelical. The truth was that Angus was probably the first non-evangelical Christian friend who I had really got to know and respect. His faith was so real it was infectious, and I loved talking to him as I felt it truly was a case of 'iron sharpening iron'.

I believe Angus is one of the main reasons I am still alive today – and I thank God for him.

It was he who – for the first time in my life – started to challenge me as to why I was so convinced that same-sex love was wrong. I remember the exact moment he brought this up. I had given him a lift into London, and we happened to be driving around an extremely busy Parliament Square. Out of the blue he asked me whether I had ever considered if there might be a different way of interpreting scripture on the issue of sexuality, and out of shock I nearly crashed the car. I remember looking over at him in astonishment, and then swerving to avoid a car that had tried to cut me up just as we approached Big Ben. An intense conversation then ensued, but I could see he truly believed that I was wrong on the matter, and I decided it was best to hear him out.

Over the weeks and months ahead, I therefore started to explore a different narrative with Angus.

Thinking about it, my life must have been more than a little challenging as I was trying to cope with the stress of my course, the reality of being in an intense friendship with Gabi, going through a lot of deliverance and prayer ministry with friends, while also exploring the scriptures with Angus. How I managed it I'm not too sure, but I do remember believing that the key was to be completely honest about what was going on inside of me. I knew from my previous breakdown that this was the only possible way through it all – to bring everything hidden into the light.

Somehow, I managed to get through the end of year exams – and in fact did rather well. It seems I was the only student on our course to achieve distinction in all four papers – international law, international politics, international trade and finance, and international diplomacy. Evidently it was a feat that few students had ever achieved – which is why I was then offered the opportunity to stay on as a Visiting Research Fellow to study international relations and religion.

Our year was quickly coming to an end. As the final course dinner approached I began to experience a surge of emotions, paramount among which was the dread of having to say goodbye to Gabi – who had become my best friend and knew me better than anyone else alive.

Fortunately, it turned out that our ending was to be prolonged as she suggested that I return with her to Romania so that she could introduce me to her country. I gladly accepted. I reasoned it would be good to have something to look forward to and thought it would also provide a chance for us to recuperate after a stressful final term. Our plan was to visit her parents in Bucharest before going off to discover the Boeheim countryside. We then planned to go off on a beach holiday somewhere warm.

Various friends begged me not to go – they thought I was making myself far too vulnerable. I disagreed. I knew and accepted that Gabi was 'just a friend' – I respected that that was all she wanted and knew that I myself could offer no more. I believed I needed to learn to enjoy the friendship for what it was, and all the life it brought (despite the pain that I alone felt).

What's more, I believed that if I wasn't to be healed then I needed to learn how to live a mandated celibate lifestyle. If

I'm honest, this felt like a lifetime prison sentence, especially given the fact that I had not received the gift of celibacy, but I recognised that if there was to be no hope of me ever having a relationship then I would have to make do with my deep friendships instead.

Celibacy and friendship – with God's grace, that would be sufficient and fulfilling for my life ahead.

<hr />

We stood in the Departure Lounge, knowing this was to be at last our final 'good bye'.

We had had a terrific few weeks – exploring Romania and then a beach holiday in Corfu. I had coped, well more or less. There had been a few blips of late night longing after an intense few days, but I repented of those immediately, and prayed for more grace. What I hadn't factored in was meeting Gabi's past boyfriend, who I must admit seemed a very present boyfriend to me – well, at least he seemed to think so. Watching the two of them together was, I'll admit it now, complete torture, and I realised that if this was indeed a trial I could think of no unkinder test.

So, there we stood. Gabi was to take a flight back to Bucharest. I to London. Both flights were virtually at the same time, so we were in Departure Lounge together. I can't remember whose flight was called first, but I do remember that it was late and hot, and that everyone was fractious.

We said our good byes. I gave Gabi a long hug and then walked towards my departure gate. Standing in the queue waiting to board I noticed a young child in front of me. She was tired and playing up. This soon developed into a full toddler tantrum in which she started to howl. I looked at her and thought how lucky she was to be able to share her emotions so freely. Suddenly, I too found tears rolling down my own cheeks. They didn't stop until I landed in London.

What to do now?

I decided the best thing was to throw myself into my Visiting Research Fellowship. I therefore started to prepare for a year that would investigate the question, 'What role did Christianity play in Tony Blair's decision to go to war with Iraq?' I had asked my friend and colleague, Bishop Michael Nazir-Ali if he would be my supervisor – which he had kindly agreed to. The Department for International Development were less sure, however, as they felt that given he was a bishop he would not be completely objective on the question! It was a foretaste of the resistance I would find in trying to get Oxford University to look at the topic of religion within international relations.

Gabi and I stayed in touch, and before long she asked if I would like to go back to Romania as she was planning to take a small group of friends to explore the Danube Delta. Naturally, I jumped at the chance. So, in early October I found myself back on a plane to Bucharest for yet another holiday. On my second day I tripped and fell. After a brief (and never to be repeated) visit to the Romanian equivalent of A & E I was told that it seemed that I had broken my ankle. I say 'seemed', as having paid for an x-ray to be taken at the hospital we then went off to see three different consultants who gave me three different opinions – each saying I had broken my ankle in three different places. Later back in Oxford it was confirmed that I had not broken it at all but had in fact badly torn some ligaments. At least the enforced bedrest did me some good.

Thankfully, I was still able to participate in the Danube Delta trip, which involved another friend from Oxford. He unfortunately had not been informed that there was a group of us, and I believe had come out thinking he was going on holiday with a woman with whom he too was deeply in love. This led to an interesting dynamic between us all – but as usual Gabi seemed oblivious to it all.

I returned to the UK, and to my research and healing. I knew that walking the tight rope of 'just being friends' was putting me under immense pressure. I wasn't too sure how long I could bear it.

———•———

By this time, I was racked by one particular question that kept haunting me through my lonely evenings at home and my long days of solitude in the library: 'Would what I desire give me the happiness I longed for, or was it a sandcastle that would disintegrate the moment I touched it?'

In other words, was what I longed and craved for – intimacy with a woman – a false desire? Was it purely a thought that had been sent to torment me and cause me great anguish; if I ever finally acted on it, would I then find myself hating it? Or was it something that I would find fulfilling and life-giving, which would bring me great joy and peace – even if it was forbidden fruit?

I so desperately wanted to know the answer to this, and yet the cost of trying to find out was so exceptionally high.

I began to think I just needed 'one experience' that would help me to know the truth. I believed it would at least bring me some peace as I would finally know the answer to who I am. But how could I find out?

———•———

Life marched relentlessly on, and the pressures just seemed to build.

In November 2007, a few days after my thirty-ninth birthday and while having my entire family to stay in Oxford – for first and only time – I was rushed into hospital with severe abdominal pain.

Tests seemed inconclusive, although the pain was excruciating. Given the NHS bed shortage I was given a bed in the Trauma ward, which was unfortunately a long way away from the Medical ward and the duty doctor who was assigned to look after me. For reasons that are still unclear I was not given any effective painkillers for three days – the Pain Control team I was informed did not work weekends, which is of course rather bad news if you are admitted like I was on a Friday night.

I thought that every part of me was screaming – my body, my head, my heart – and by the end of it all my very soul. I had had enough. I was in agony, and it seemed that no one was able to help.

I ended up staying in hospital for nearly ten days, while they ran some MRI tests and considered whether it might be worth operating. The doctors were split on a diagnosis – some thought it was my gallbladder and that I had been passing gallstones (even though they couldn't see any). Others were less sure. I remember one young doctor coming to see me and saying that he thought my body was suffering acute stress. He asked me whether I thought that might be a factor? I did.

I was eventually put on a high level of painkillers and discharged without a clear diagnosis. A few months later my GP suggested that I might want to go back on antidepressants as I was finding life increasingly hard to 'keep on keeping on'. I wasn't sleeping, my memory was terrible, I was tired all the time and I was incredibly low. He and I both knew I would never take my own life, but even so I was constantly haunted by the thought that dying would be a welcome solution, as it would remove me from this state of utter hopelessness. I knew that wasn't a healthy or normal state of mind, but at the same time the battle of day to day living just seemed too much.

I was beside myself with what to do – knowing only too well what the root cause of it all was.

And of course, deep down there were always the unspoken questions of 'Where is God in all this? Why is He refusing to answer my prayers? What have I done to bring on all this pain? Why am I being tested so much, and will it ever, ever end?' I say unspoken, although the truth was that the thoughts ran screaming through my head incessantly – day and night. Especially the night.

On all these matters, though, God remained completely silent.

———•———

I buried myself in my research and made the added decision to attend every lecture on Politics, Philosophy and International Relations that I could get to – plus a little bit of Theology thrown in for good measure. I reasoned that if I was to self-fund an additional year, then I might as well get as much out of it as I could. Studying at least took my mind off things, and there was so much one could learn – especially at Oxford, where there was a plethora of international lectures each term.

In fact, I can highly recommend taking a year out to study if you possibly can. The joy of learning for pure interest's sake – not because one has to, or because one has an exam to pass, but just because one wants to. I consumed whole courses willingly – much to the amazement of the undergraduates around me who couldn't believe I was attending 9 a.m. lectures out of choice.

By now, my research had gone off in a rather unusual direction. Given I was self-financing I had been pretty much left to my own devices, so I decided to follow my gut and 'go wherever the research trail took me'. As I had explained to the department head, I had been an ardent critic of Tony Blair while on the Archbishops' Council, which I happened to be on during the run up to the Iraq War. As such, I had been party to various private letters between Tony and the Archbishops,[1]

[1] Both George Carey and Rowan Williams were involved in trying to dissuade him from going to war with Iraq

and had also been across many of the realities on the ground, thanks to my work with Canon Andrew White. As far as I could tell numerous decisions and statements just didn't add-up, and I began to believe there was a completely different narrative that we, the British public, weren't being told.

At the same time, I found myself being drawn into the Intelligence Community at Oxford, which happened to be a mecca for retired spooks. This was primarily thanks to two intelligence groups that held evening lecturers and dinners, and which I had been invited to join when I had been part of the Foreign Service Programme. These evenings were fascinating and gave me access to a range of senior intelligence officials – both past and present – from across the services.

I found myself investigating the nature of the 'special relationship' between the UK and the US. Fortunately, Edward Snowden blew the whistle on most of what I was researching a few years ago in the *Guardian*, although arguably I believe there is still far more to be uncovered. Who'd have thought that within five years of doing this research, that I would be working for Mr Blair himself as a Director of his Faith Foundation? He was a man I had – through my research – developed a great respect for, and who I can personally testify to be a man of deep faith and integrity.

Evidently it can take just one straw to break a camel's back.

I can well believe it – for that's all that it took to break me too.

In Easter 2008 I made a third and final trip to Romania. At Gabi's suggestion I had actually been considering relocating over there to write a book as her parents had a second home on Lake Snagov, a perfect retreat for such a task. The relocation was not to be, however, as Gabi was awarded a scholarship to do a Masters at Columbia University in New York. So I put my

Romanian plans on hold and agreed to go and visit her in the Big Bad Apple later that year.

We therefore planned my trip for late October, just before my fortieth birthday. Despite all the fun of being in New York for Halloween and the Marathon, Gabi could tell I was seriously low.

On my last night, Gabi had an essay crisis, so I decided to go out and explore The Village District, hoping to find a lesbian bar where I might try and meet someone. I obviously wasn't in the right place – as I couldn't find any, so I went back to Times Square and spent the evening in the Irish Pub. Gabi took me back to the Village the next evening for our last meal together before I left to catch my flight. Ironically, it was therefore in a lesbian bar that she told me she didn't think we should meet again. She was painfully aware of the agony she was causing me, and despite our best efforts at 'just being friends' she could see it was making me desperately unhappy.

So, she did what I had not had the courage to do – she cut the umbilical cord.

I was more than heartbroken. I was devastated. Distraught. Driven to distraction with desire for something I thought was evil and wrong and sinful, and yet something which I could not change.

Something had to give – otherwise my life was only going to get darker, and I knew I would not survive. The first, the most important step had to be to find out who I truly was.

The only logical thing I could think of doing was to date some guys and date some girls and see how I felt about the differing experiences. This was a world I knew virtually nothing about. I was 'fresh (and very naïve) meat.' Indeed, if it wasn't for a man who kindly realised this and decided to protect me by explaining the dangers of online dating, I'm not sure what would have happened.

I learnt a lot over the following two months, not least about the differing natures of men and women. I was left without any doubt that I was definitely attracted to women, with whom I could make far deeper and more real connections – emotionally, mentally, spiritually and physically.

But my final straw?

Despite what you might think, it was not Gabi cutting the cord, but in fact the Church choosing to do so. Just before Christmas I finally got to see the Director of 'Pastoral Care' in our church, who I had been trying to see for some time. In tears I explained that I could no longer cope. I had tried everything – I had done all that I had been asked to do by the Church. I had submitted myself to every form of prayer and deliverance I could find, and yet I was still left with these unwanted feelings and a longing for love that was ungodly, and which I believed could never be met.

I remember him looking up at me across his desk, nodding and simply saying: 'I believe this is a matter for just you and God, Jayne, no one else can help you now.'

Boom. The door was shut.

I was crying for help – for a life line, for a way out of my darkness. But the door was slammed shut in my face. I was left alone to work it out with my Maker – the Church had nothing more to say.

This time there was no light around the door frame to show me there was any sign of hope.

And so, I made a decision that would change my life. A decision that I knew would cost me everything. A decision, not based on theological conviction or a word from God, but on a pure and simple desire to keep on breathing. I felt I had been left with no option. If I wanted to live I needed to find a different path. The tunnel I was in no longer had a light at the end of it. In fact, it just seemed to be taking me down into deeper darkness – and towards certain death.

Back to School

I reasoned that if God truly loved me then He would forgive me, even if I was walking away from His plan for me. I reckoned He knew how hard I had tried and that even if I had failed the test He had set, He must surely somehow continue to love me and forgive me. That's what unconditional love means, doesn't it? However, I knew my biggest challenge would be coming to grips with my own sense of failure and knowing that those around me would also find that impossible to do too.

CHAPTER TWELVE

Just Loving

January 2009

There she was! I could see her clearly now – she was even more beautiful than her online photo.

As agreed she was waiting by the entrance to the National Portrait Gallery, standing tall and elegant, with her long brown hair flowing down over her full-length fur coat (faux, I rightly presumed) and pulling her collar tightly round her for warmth given how bitterly cold it was.

I gulped and stepped up the pace – she hadn't spotted me yet, and I so hated being late. The traffic from Oxford had been a nightmare, and we'd therefore had to rearrange our meeting venue twice whilst I was en route. Fortunately, I had managed to get through to the Portrait restaurant, and they had kindly said they would fit us in if we could get there within the next thirty minutes.

And then it dawned on me – this wonderful, tall, attractive, intelligent woman was standing there waiting for *me*! I mean, she was there because she *wanted* to meet *me* – just as much as I wanted to meet her. We were about to embark on 'a date' – and I suddenly felt incredibly nervous.

It is a relatively short walk down Charing Cross Road from Leicester Square, but my legs began to feel exceptionally heavy. The ghosts of my past started to swirl around me, and the voice of whatever animal it is that perches on our shoulder telling us all the things that we fear the most, became deafening: that I was undesirable, unattractive, inexperienced, out of my depth ….

Just Loving

And then she saw me and smiled. We both laughed – well giggled really, just like school girls.

That was the start of the most beautiful day of my life – a day that lasted five and a half years.

A month or so later we were heading back home from our first Valentine's Day trip away. It had been a magical few days, not least because of what we knew it represented for both of us – a decision of clear commitment in the midst of what had become a whirlwind romance.

Vienna had always been my fairy tale destination, and it seemed so fitting when we'd both said we wanted to go there for our first holiday together. How ironic I thought that I had eventually ended up going there with my first love, rather than moving there with Kimberly-Clark all those years ago.

So, we had kissed in front of Klimt's *The Kiss*, eaten Sacher-Torte in Café Sacher, toured the Opera House, visited both the Summer and Winter Palaces – and even found a lesbian bar.

But sitting on the plane on our way home, my head was in turmoil. How on earth was I going to manage this? What was I going to tell people? *How* was I going to tell people? I was so happy – so alive, and yet I still believed I was walking away from God and from all that I had been called to.

Sensing my disquiet, Lizzie had taken my hand. And there we sat – a couple so obviously in love.

My primary goal had been to find out who I was, and whether being in a relationship with a woman would make me happy. I had no doubt now that I was gay, and that yes, it most certainly did make me happy. But I hadn't thought beyond that – what would I do next? How did someone with my background 'come out'? Indeed, I had only just started coming out to myself.

We were sat in a row of three seats, Lizzie by the window

and I in the middle. The seat next to me was free and looking around the full flight I realised we were the lucky ones – we seemed to have the only spare seat left on the plane. I was about to get up and move to the aisle seat to give us a bit more room, when there was a noise at the front of the plane and the final passenger boarded. I looked up and saw a middle-aged man, dressed completely in black, with a white square just below his chin. I sank back into my seat, sensing with dread that he was headed straight for us.

I tried to let go of Lizzie's hand, but she just grabbed it even more tightly and winked at me. I wanted to explain: 'You just don't understand!', but this was neither the time nor the place.

Sitting down next to me, the relieved clergyman told us that he thought he'd missed his flight. He busied himself getting his things sorted and then turned to me and said, 'I know you, don't I?'

'Not now, Lord, not here!' was all I could think, still trying to extricate myself from Lizzie's hand.

To this day I've no idea who this Anglican priest was. He did give me a few clues, but when I looked him up later they didn't seem to lead anywhere. I now even wonder if he was an angel.[1]

Whoever he was, I'm so very grateful for the way he so carefully steered the conversation throughout our ninety-minute flight. He obviously had recognised me and had quickly worked out the whole situation. He shared in depth about his own difficult family situation of having a daughter who was beset with mental health problems, and who his own church had continuously prayed for until they got too frustrated that nothing was happening. They had then started blaming him and his wife for her lack of healing, and that it was 'obviously'

[1] But if you are real, and are reading this – please, please do get in touch so I can say thank you!

because of some unrepented sin. He and the family had all been very hurt and they had eventually moved away, knowing that God was calling them to love their child just as she was – not as others thought she should be.

I listened attentively – grateful and incredulous that I was sitting next to someone who seemed to be sharing a story so pertinent to my own, so freely and so unexpectedly. Towards the end of the flight he asked if I had ever heard of the Revd Dr Michael Vasey? No, I explained, I had not. He then took out his pen and wrote down '*Strangers and Friends* by the Revd Dr Michael Vasey'. Handing the piece of paper to me, he urged me to get hold of a copy and read it: 'You'll know you're not alone!'

That book was a life line.

I so wish I had had the privilege of meeting Dr Vasey before he died of an AIDS-related illness in 1998. He was an evangelical who had taught at both St John's Theological College and Cranmer Hall, Durham, and who wrote this extraordinarily brave book about homosexuality and the Church.

My vicar friend was right – I was not alone. There were others! There were others with deep faith who understood the trauma I had gone through, and who had accepted who they were in Christ.

I began to hope.

Thanks to the internet and references in the book I learnt of an evangelical LGBTI ministry called Courage, led by a wonderful man called Jeremy Marks. It may seem strange, but I couldn't bring myself to get in touch with him at first – I was too scared. Instead, I read everything on his website and started numerous emails which I then deleted. I realised it would mean going back into the horrid mess of trying to reconcile everything, and quite frankly I was just loving being 'in the real world' and 'being loved' by someone who had no hang ups with the Church.

But I knew that this new bubble couldn't last and that I

would have to 'come out' to my family and friends at some point – that is, so long as I wasn't outed first, which was another constant fear.

Obviously for Lizzie things were quite different. Within a couple of weeks of our meeting I had met her entire family, helped somewhat by an unexpected cold spell which brought severe snow to the South East. This had thrown us together far quicker than I had envisaged or was ready for.

There are many losses I've had to come to terms with over the years because of my inner conflict with my faith and sexuality – some more profound than others. From quite early on I had come to accept that I was very unlikely to have my own children, a fact that I have only recently had time to think about and grieve. As much as I would have loved to have been a mum, I recognised that my single lifestyle precluded this. I have always hoped I might meet someone with children – who knows, maybe I still will one day. One thing is certain, I won't now be having children of my own.

At this particular time, however, it was the simple disappointment of not being able to share the excitement of meeting my other half's parents for the first time that saddened me most. I had memories of my sister and close friends ringing me excitedly before their own encounters, and I so desperately wanted to be able to do the same. It was a significant milestone for me – Lizzie *wanted* me to meet them, and I was excited and petrified all at the same time. But I realised that this too was a path that I would have to walk alone. Indeed, sometimes there are things that only God can witness with us, even if we yearn for others to do so.

And of course, I wanted Lizzie to meet *my* parents ....

I decided the best course of action was for them to meet her initially just as my friend – someone who I had got to know recently, and who I enjoyed spending time with. For the first time in years I therefore asked if I could bring a friend home with me to Guernsey for Easter, which they readily agreed to. I can't remember how I had said we knew each other – friends of friends I think.

Lizzie was a hit! Her wit and charm had them in stitches from the moment we landed, and I could see my parents had taken her into their hearts immediately. They kept remarking how happy and relaxed I seemed, and what a changed person I appeared to be in her company – a point which my mother made privately to Lizzie just before we boarded our flight back to London.

After some intense discussion, we decided that they must have guessed – the comments were just too pointed, and my happiness just too apparent. So, I wrote and told them the truth – explaining that I was pleased that they had had a chance to meet the one woman who had brought so much light and joy into my life. I explained I had finally found peace, and with it true happiness. I had told them of my inner conflict at various key points over the years, but it was never something we had discussed – save once with Angus, where my mother had just said 'but it's so clearly wrong!'

It was a major step for me – and at the time, as I was soon to learn, a step too far for them.

The follow-up phone call with them both wasn't easy. Sadly, the words I remember most, which cut right through me, were 'we're very disappointed'. I later understood this to mean they were disappointed they wouldn't have any grandchildren. 'Join the club!' was all I could think.

Every LGBT person I have ever met has a coming out story to tell – even if it's simply coming out to ourselves. The hardest thing is always to tell those we love, especially when we're unsure of how they will react. Our default position is normally to assume that they will react badly – which is why we often decide to hold back. However, sometimes it goes surprisingly well; although there are of course times when it is a complete unmitigated disaster. Sometimes we are outed against our will; other times we find ourselves longing to be outed – desperate for someone to say something that will enable us to admit: 'yes, it's true'. Sometimes it ends in a hug; sometimes it ends in harsh words and a slammed door. We can never tell. The important thing is that we've owned our truth, and we are no longer having to hide. You see – the truth will *always* set us free.

However, once the truth is out, then people have a choice that only they can make. Either they start a journey – which is not one they would have chosen, or one they expected, but one out of love that they know they must make, for love's sake. Or instead they close the door; unsure of what to say – so they say nothing; unsure of what to do – so they do nothing. And in so doing they build a wall out of inaction and silence, through which no redeeming love can easily penetrate.

Those who have chosen to embark on this journey know it takes time, patience and love – lots of love. Lots of *unconditional* love. Forgiveness too, on both sides, especially for words unwisely said.

However, for those who choose to stay put just where they are, who choose to withdraw and remain silent, this too is done by making a clear decision. For most believe that they are being called to choose between the friend or relative they love and being true to a 'greater love'.

This is the ultimate oxymoron – that this 'greater love', which is out of obedience to their God of Love, demands that they withhold their love from someone because of their innate desire *to* love. So, they cut the cord, they close the door and they refuse to give their love and blessing.

I am proud to say that my parents, unlike many named in this book, chose to start this journey. It would take them on different routes and they would arrive at different places at different times, but they have both bravely walked it – and so they came to fully embrace Lizzie and I over the years.

I understand that the greatest factor in their journey was the obvious and tangible difference that her love had made to my life. I was so obviously fully alive! I was happy! I looked different, I sounded different, I acted different. I was filled with joy, and happiness, and peace, and hope.

Most of all – hope. There was light back in my eyes!

So now they knew.

I just had the rest of the evangelical church to tell – including most of my closest friends.

One of the questions that was beginning to dawn on me was: 'Is my coming out going to be news?' It hadn't occurred to me for a moment that it would be, given it had been over four years since I had been on the Archbishops' Council. However, the reaction of the vicar on the plane and the constant outings of public figures in the news had led me to recognise that the media had an unhealthy interest in anything that could link 'Church', 'sex' and 'sexuality' in one sentence.

I also had no idea how the evangelical world was going to react. Would I be publicly humiliated and rejected? Would there be a public disassociation from me? I was still in touch with many senior evangelicals – some of whom formed the most vocal part of the anti-gay lobby in the UK.

And then I began to think of all the people who would be clearly hurt by the news – close friends, mentors, colleagues and past prayer warriors. I had a couple of evangelical friends who were still supporting me financially as I had yet to find any doors opening after my time at Oxford. I knew I needed to tell them urgently – and find a way of somehow offering to pay them back.

Just Love

This was a mess, and I had no idea how to deal with it.

I lay back in bed, still reeling from the conversation with my parents, and listened to the *Today Programme* whilst Lizzie got ready for work. The *Thought for the Day* reflection was always worth a listen, and so I tried to make a point of tuning in – just in case it had a lifeline of hope for my situation.

It was Bishop James Jones – an old friend from Council days. His voice so familiar and yet so distant, memories of a bygone era which now seemed a lifetime away. My mind started to wander, and I remembered our heated conversations over the Listening Programme. Luckily it had finally led to the *Restoring Hope in Our Church* project being formed. And then I remembered that he had spoken out – just over a year before, whilst I was going through all my angst with Gabi – about the need for evangelicals to think again about their attitude to homosexuality.

I sat up, reached for my iPad and started Googling. It didn't take me long to find the lecture that had hit the news entitled 'Making Space for Grace and Truth'. I realised immediately that he was someone who would understand. All I needed to do was to get hold of him – so I looked up an email address for him, courtesy of his diocese, and fired off an email asking if there was any way we might possibly be able to meet as I wanted to ask his advice on something confidential and urgent. It was a shot in the dark, but it was all that I had – and somehow, I felt it was meant to be.

A week or so later I was sat in an armchair near the window of one of the bars in the House of Lords, looking out over the Thames. Bishop James had been so gracious – he happened to be in London as he was duty bishop in the House of Lords and somehow, he had managed to clear some time in his diary to meet. He must have wondered why I had written with such seeming urgency, but he didn't say anything – he just poured the tea and sat back waiting for me to explain.

This was it, I thought. If I told Bishop James about it all then there would be no going back.

Just Loving

I stumbled through the events of the past few years, trying my best to explain the utter confusion and pain I had been in. Even there, even then – knowing what he had so clearly written – I was still scared to explain who or rather what I was, fearful of the consequences and of rejection.

But he was brilliant – un-fazed, un-shocked and wonderfully pastoral.

We talked through whether this would be news, and he felt the media would respect the fact that I had now stepped down from my public role, and that I was therefore 'off limits'. He did however feel it was important for me to take ownership of my own story and advised me that I should look to tell it myself – otherwise others would do so for me. He suggested that I consider writing a letter, in my own words explaining the journey I had been on and the reasons for the decision I had felt that I'd been left with no choice but to make. His recommendation was that I then send it to all my senior evangelical friends at the same time as my past Council colleagues.

Towards the end of our meeting he asked if I had a diary or a notebook to hand. Perplexed, I handed him the little leather-bound notebook that I always carried with me. He took out his fountain pen and began to write – a prayer, he explained, which he felt sure was meant for me.

It was the Prayer of King Henry VI. It sits on my desk, worn, battered and ever-so-much cherished:

O Lord Jesus Christ,
Who hast created and redeemed me
And hast brought me unto that which now I am: [heavily underlined]
Thou knowest what Thou wouldest do with me:
Do with me according to Thy will, for Thy tender mercy's sake.
Amen

I looked at it, read it and the tears began to fall. I looked up and saw that his eyes were moist too.

I will never ever forget that meeting. I've sat in that room numerous times with many members of the House of Lords. I've helped entertain key movers and shakers from around the world, but this was the most significant meeting I have had, or will ever have, there.

I am in no doubt that the meeting was both God-ordained and God-sanctioned. It was a blessing and an absolution – from a man I deeply admired, respected and trusted. As I still do.

I felt a crushing weight had finally been lifted, and yet I knew my real journey had only just begun.

I say, 'real journey', it's just that deep down I knew – and if I'm honest, I had always known without daring to believe – that this was my true calling. It had been no 'coincidence' that I had got on to the Archbishops' Council just after my first breakdown, that I had then forged key relationships with so many well-known evangelicals, at the same time as struggling with my sexuality, and that I had tried every possible form of healing. This was all part of 'the great big plan' for my life, independent of whether I wanted it or not. It was what I had been born for.

This would start another major battle in my head – and one that would form the nub of my most heated discussions with Mr God over the next five years. I did not want to go back to living by faith. Never, ever, again. No. Not ever. It was too stressful, too costly. Surely, I deserved a wage like everyone else? I wanted stability and normality – so no, I was just not going to do it.

Just Loving

You might now be asking, where was I with God and my faith? Had I just abandoned it all in my seemingly selfish quest for love?

The reality was that, despite what I had been taught – that I was living in the deepest and darkest of sin and walking away from all that God had for me – I felt closer to God than I had ever done before. He was still there in my thoughts, in my dreams, whispering in my inner ear – providing checks in my spirit, and showing me the way ahead. To begin with I had completely doubted it was Him. But then after the man on the plane and various other small 'coincidences' I began thinking that maybe, just maybe, God had not changed one tiny jot towards me. The Church might have done, yes, but that was another story – and one that would take a lifetime to change.

God was still the same. I was still the same – well, no, I was now completely transformed, by love!

———— •—• ————

I wrote the letter as Bishop James suggested and met with him a month or so later to discuss it in more depth. Like, him, I believed it was important that I got the tone right – I didn't want it to be an overly emotional letter, but one that clearly and factually set out the path I had been on and the reasons for the decisions I had made. He was very complimentary and said he wouldn't change a word. We then talked through its ramifications, and what it might mean for me.

I had already stopped going to St Aldates – it was just too painful. I had tried going to a New Wine Women's event at Westminster Central Hall where I had found myself being prayed for by Ann Coles. She was deeply disturbed when I shared that I was in love with a woman, and I knew I was now in such a different place that it would only continue to cause me great anguish if I tried to stay in the evangelical charismatic world. Our understanding of the nature of God, particularly whether He was there wanting to embrace all or just those who lived by a certain code, was just too far apart. I was not going to repent of something I did not believe needed repenting of, nor was I going to buy into the misguided belief that LGBTI people should remain celibate.

I drew up a list of who the letter should go to, printed off the requisite number of copies and posted them all at the same time. I had marked the letter 'Strictly Private and Confidential', which I thought they would honour. However, given I had included a distribution list I assumed they would talk to each other. I thought that word would inevitably get out. On that I was wrong.

———— • ————

My first reply, just three days later, came in a crisp yellow envelope with a House of Lords seal on the back. I ripped it open and paused when I saw the name of the Archbishop who I had worked so closely with whilst on the Archbishops' Council. I had added a personal footnote to his letter, apologising to him for the disappointment I feared the contents would bring. I knew that he had placed great faith in me publicly throughout our years together on Council, and I was deeply aware of how this news might affect him – and indeed be used against him if the media got hold of it.

My tear stains are still obvious on his reply – forming dark blotches as I read his kind and deeply pastoral words, which meant more to me than he will ever know. 'My dear, dear Jayne … NO your decision has not disappointed me. Surprised me yes …'. It is a private letter, and one that I hope I myself might have the wisdom and grace to write if ever I needed to. It left me in no doubt that I was loved and cherished by both him and his wife and showed great sensitivity and insight about the challenges I would now face. The phrase I remember most was his imploring me to 'not give up on the Church' and ending with the reminder that Moses' ministry began when he was 40+.

Other letters followed, mostly from those who I knew would understand and 'be on side'. Then there was a long pause. And finally, my two closest Archbishops' Council friends, both senior conservative evangelicals, wrote in their own time and in their own way. They each had obviously struggled with the dichotomy of showing their sincere love for me as a person and yet their deep concern for my soul, but at least they had the courage to try – and I respect and love them for it. They knew I would disagree, but they felt beholden to tell me the truth as they saw it as they were so worried for me. I have met with both to try and talk about it; we have had to agree to disagree.

The rest remained silent – and to this day I have not heard from most of them, neither those with whom I had been so close nor those from the wider evangelical world. It is always the silence that hurts the most, especially from people you regarded as your closest friends. I remember my friend Angela Tilby once saying to me that I should take their silence as a mark of respect – that people were obviously confounded about what to say and so said nothing. Personally, I would have rather they had tried – as it's impossible to engage with silence, but instead one reads into it a million different things.

I used the same letter over the weeks and months ahead to tell my various family members and friends. I thought it best to 'stick to the script', yet each time I sent a letter my heart immediately ached to know what they would think and how they would react. 'Who else has to do this?' I kept asking myself. It was self-inflicted torture. But then I realised that there was, sadly, no other way.

One morning I was preparing some coffee when my mobile phone rang. I saw from the screen that it was my godmother – my mother's closest sister. I had recently sent her the letter, although I was convinced she already knew the news as I was sure my mother would have spoken to her at length. I hesitated to answer, not knowing what she was going to say – the constant knocks of rejection had been hitting me hard, and I was realising I wasn't quite as resilient as I thought I was.

'Darling, I'm just ringing to apologise', she said, as soon as I answered.

Taken off guard, I asked what on earth she was apologising for?

'Dearest Jayne, we've always known, ever since you were a little girl – I just wish that we had had the courage to talk to you about it, and I'm so, so sorry given all you've had to go through!'

Even now it's difficult to find words to express the range of emotions that coursed through me – utter relief, deep sorrow, gratefulness, confusion, and anger. It was the anger that lingered – why hadn't anyone ever said anything? It had taken me more than forty years to find out what others had evidently always known – but their silence had nearly killed me. That said, I was very grateful to my aunt for finding the courage to tell me, even if after all these years. She too has been a lifeline.

I've since started to appreciate the phrase 'hidden in clear sight' and I now realise that there are many things that we can all see and know, but we do not talk about. Putting it bluntly, many parents know that their children are gay – often before the child has even learnt to spell their own name. They can tell by the way they interact with others, who and what they play with, or who they are drawn towards. Of course, it is always dangerous to stereo-type, but at the same time we should never ignore what is plainly obvious for all to see – even if it is an inconvenient truth.

Just Loving

So, 2009 was proving quite a year. I was by now renting my house out to ensure I had some form of income. My numerous job applications were not going well, which, given the emotional rollercoaster I was on, was probably just as well – even if it wasn't at all good for the bank balance.

I knew I needed a break – a complete break, where I could get away from the stress of it all. I wanted to be able to breathe freely – and I needed air. Lizzie was also keen for a sabbatical, having worked relentlessly for years as co-owner of her family firm. So, we plotted our escape, and on hearing the unexpected news that a family wanted to rent my house for a few months, we bit the bullet and announced we were going 'Down Under' for a two-month trip of a lifetime.

These have, without doubt, to be the happiest days of my life.

Free from everything and everyone – we both relaxed into being 'just us' and enjoying our new life together. Boy did we have some adventures – Japan, Australia, New Zealand and Hong Kong.

It showed me what being wedded to someone – body, mind and spirit – was all about. It made me believe that we were truly destined for each other, and that we could live through anything. I was, sadly, going to find I was wrong about that, but at least at the time I started dreaming of the future, and realising that love is something that acts as the most healing medicine of all.

It is often said that you remember people by how they make you feel – and I remember feeling happy! To be fair, I don't think I've ever laughed so much as I did with Lizzie. We were good sparring partners – both with quick wits and with a similar sense of humour. Really important in any relationship.

There was one day though when we were taken off guard, and both of us lost our sense of humour. We were staying with a lesbian couple in the Blue Mountains outside of Sydney. They were related to a couple of good friends whose wedding blessing we had gone out for. I had played a significant part in their actual wedding in Cambridge (a sort of 'best woman' role); it had been our first 'official function' together, and it meant so much to be invited as a couple.

Thinking back, it was the first time we had ever met or spent time with another lesbian couple and talk naturally came around to stories of 'coming out' and our past. After what was quite an intense discussion, one of our hosts braved saying something to us which certainly knocked me for six. I am so glad she did though. In a nutshell, she challenged us as to whether we had ever recognised our own internalised homophobia – a very common factor for those who have struggled to come out because of prejudice and stigma within their immediate communities.

'Homophobic?! Me?' was all I could think, and I think Lizzie probably felt the same. Had they no idea what I had gone through to come out? How could I still be called homophobic?

But I realised, after a period of reflection, that she had a point. There was something within me that did not want to be associated with LGBTI people. Lizzie and I just happened to be two women in love. It may sound strange, but I never thought of us as two lesbians. Just two people in love.

I didn't quite know what to do, but I felt that the best thing would be to repent in good evangelical style and to ask God to forgive me and free me of anything that was homophobic in my spirit.

Now this is the critical thing, which I wish so many of my evangelical friends could understand.

The moment I did that, I felt the vestiges of the inner conflicting voices immediately disappear. Up to that point I had continued to feel tormented 'in my spirit' that I was – despite what I knew in my head and my heart – living contrary to the will of God. To non-evangelicals this may not make too much sense, but so much of my life to that point had been determined by 'the witness in my spirit' of what I believed was the Holy Spirit. I just 'knew in my knower' that some things were either right or wrong. It's what makes so many godly people, despite all the evidence they are presented with, continue to believe that same-sex relationships are wrong – they just say that 'they know'. So, my testimony here is that the moment I broke that homophobic spirit off me – the one spirit that I should always have had deliverance from – my inner spiritual life changed.

And I finally found peace.

———•———

At the end of January 2010, we rather reluctantly returned to the UK. There were moments when we had seriously considered staying out there, and I know part of me will always wish we had.

On the journey home I began to think of my next chapter. How was I going to get a job? What could I do? I needed something to pay off the holiday, but no Christian organisation wanted to touch me, and I had learnt the hard way that secular groups thought my CV 'too religious'.

Standing in the arrivals hall of Heathrow Terminal 5, I turned my phone on and checked my emails. There in my Inbox was an email from a head hunter (who I didn't know) wondering if I might like to talk to her about a maternity cover post as Director of Fund Development for the Worldwide Association of Girl Guides. They were just about to enter their centenary year, during which they wanted to launch the Global Girls Fund, and were urgently needing to appoint someone who was familiar with the international development scene and, well, wasn't fundraising the same as marketing?

I started at the World Bureau in Hampstead a few weeks later.

These coincidences would keep coming – jobs over the next few years would follow one after the other. God was still on my case, even if there were nail-biting periods where I was left hanging, wondering if and when any help would come.

You see, I've never had any difficulty believing God *can* do something, it's just whether He *will* do something *this time* that has always worried me.

———— • ————

But what about Church?

In truth, I felt I was living in total exile.

After my initial coming out, I had likened life to being in a desert – a dry and lonely place where I felt I had been taken. But then I realised that I had, as yet, no hope of a Promised Land – and that I had in effect been made to leave my home country, which I so desperately wanted to return to.

Lizzie and I did try a few churches together, but none where we felt really welcomed. It was quite noticeable going back to some evangelical churches that we were left alone, almost as lepers – seats around us were left free, people who would normally come and hug me hello would turn and find someone else to talk to. No one said anything to us directly, but their silence spoke volumes. We were being tolerated, and yet we wanted to be warmly welcomed and included.

One of the greatest blessings that Lizzie brought to my life was the fact that her faith was so real, even if she didn't feel comfortable with organised religion. Like so many of my LGBTI friends, the Church was the last place she expected to be welcomed. Having said that fortunately she did have a positive experience the one time she took her parents to Midnight Mass one Christmas Eve. For a reason only known to the vicar, he had welcomed everybody at the start of the service and extended a particularly warm welcome to anyone from the LGBTI community, apologising for the way the Church of England might have made them feel during the year. God bless him!

Lizzie *knew* the nature of God, I often thought better than I did myself – and would constantly remind me of His unconditional love at times I needed to hear it most. I remember her often commenting on things that had been said to me: 'But that's not the God you and I know, Jayne', which was exactly what I needed to hear so often after a painful letter or email. It meant so much that we prayed together, and celebrated God's love in our lives – even if others couldn't.

Eventually we just gave up going anywhere, and I found myself becoming increasingly weary and cynical of anything to do with church. It seemed to be the source of such pain and division, and quite frankly I'd had enough. There was part of me that wondered if Jesus was still going too.

———— •—

Our relationship had hit some rocky ground, which is perhaps not surprising when you take two middle-aged women who have never been in a long-term relationship before and throw them together with minimal support. I was therefore back in Oxford on one of our 'mini-breaks'.

Nursing my hurting heart, I found myself living for weeks on end in complete solitude and silence. Our break up had unfortunately only brought relief to some of my family and evangelical friends, who ventured to tell me that it was God's judgement on my life for having been living in sin. Not much comfort there, sadly. At least there were some kind neighbours, who became very dear friends.

And then there was Margreet.

Thank God for Margreet! She had started as the vicar of our little struggling, desperately poor parish church in Littlemore about the same time as I moved in to the area, but I hadn't really got to know her. Given I live right next door to the Village Hall, I found myself bumping into her every so often as she helped with various community groups. One day, seeing me looking extremely low, she asked if I'd like her to pop round for a visit. I said that that would be lovely, and then immediately panicked thinking – how am I going to explain all that's been going on?

Tea with Margreet was a God-send and yet another

lifeline. She sat and listened as I poured out my anger and pain, and my utter confusion as to where God was in all of this. She recommended various books to me to read – often old favourites that I had long time forgotten – such as Gerard W. Hughes, Henri Nouwen and Jean Vanier. Slowly, lovingly and prayerfully she nursed me back to life. Finally, at the end of the year, she invited me to play in the Community Carol Service.

Which is how I – well actually, we (as we had by now got back together) – got involved with Littlemore, the church built by John Henry Newman and from which he preached his last Anglican sermon. I've often thought his story quite like mine – especially as I have strong reason to believe we were dealing with the same inner conflicts, and as a result journeyed the same spiritual path.

Our first Sunday together at Littlemore couldn't have been more different from those aborted attempts elsewhere. The church may not have running water, toilets or heating, but it has gallons and gallons of unconditional love. It is a community of all sorts – people from every walk of life, where all are welcome for just who they are. At the end of the service, an elderly lady in the pew in front of us turned around and said: 'So good to see you Jayne, is this your partner, can I meet her?'

Taken off guard, and not knowing how to reply, I paused and looked at Lizzie. I then felt a warm touch on my hand from this wonderful woman of God, who said: 'It's okay dear, I do understand, my husband became a woman just before he died.' I took her hand and started to cry, we all did.

I had come home. We had come home.

It was such a different style of church to what I had been used to but, remembering the sermon I preached at John Coles' church all those years ago about willingly serving the churches near to us, I gave myself to Littlemore and served it as best I could. Whether it was playing my violin to lead the singing when our organist was ill or trying to get some money for simple things like a water dispenser, so the tea ladies didn't have to walk to the standing pipe in the rain, I did what I could.

I also joined Christ Church Cathedral Singers, and so found myself just a few yards physically – but a million miles liturgically – from St Aldates singing Choral Evensong every so often.

———————

Life is complicated though, and things never quite work out the way we would like them to.

Sadly, Lizzie and I, after a good run of many wonderful years together realised there were some difficulties and differences that we couldn't surmount. So, in June 2014 we decided finally to part.

———————

Splitting up is never easy.

For me it involved one small and ever so painful act – arguably it's the hardest thing I've ever had to do.

I share it here because in many ways it sums up the rollercoaster ride of being in love. The joy and the sorrow of loving, of risking it all and losing it all, but being grateful for the journey all the same.

After I picked up the last of my things, I drove down the A20 and headed straight for Bluewater. I parked in our usual car park and retraced the familiar steps to a shop I'd been in a month or so earlier.

Taking out the little square box from my handbag, I placed it on the counter and pushed it towards the sales assistant. 'I'd like to bring this back, please' I said quietly, 'I've still got the receipt.'

The lady opened the box and stared down at its contents, checking it hadn't been damaged or worn. 'Is there anything wrong with it?' she asked innocently.

Just Love

I started to tremble and bit my lip hard. I gently shook my head and gave a small shrug.

She was about the same age as me, and I noted that she was wearing a similar ring to the one in the box. I caught her eye and she gave me one of the kindest smiles that said she understood.

I welled up. I knew I wasn't going to hold it together much longer – I had to get out of there, and fast. I bowed my head and stared at the credit card machine, focusing intently on what she was doing. How long could it take? Finally, I scribbled my name and address on the receipt, collected my card and literally ran out of the shop into the ladies' toilets that were just along the corridor.

It took me some time to compose myself – years of un-cried tears seemed to appear from nowhere, cascading in a flood as if the dam had finally burst and would go on forever.

They eventually stopped – they always do.

I took a deep breath in and as I did so recognised that old familiar feeling of being back to being 'just me', a single woman on her own again in the world. Alone, yes, but somehow this time it was different. I dried my eyes, checked my hair and walked out into the busy shopping centre.

'At least,' I thought to myself, 'now I know that Tennyson was right. 'Tis definitely better to have loved and lost, than never to have loved at all.'

I had loved and been loved.

I hope that maybe one day, God willing, I might do so again.

It's how we've been created – and it is the most natural desire in the world!

For all I had ever wanted, indeed all I still ever want – is to JUST LOVE.

Postscript

August 2014

On 14 August 2014, just a few weeks after I had finally settled back into Oxford, a well-known evangelical made the unprecedented move of 'coming out' in an exclusive newspaper interview.

How did I know? Because various friends texted me – several of whom I hadn't heard from for years – and asked if I'd seen the article. Vicky Beeching's story[2], it seems, appeared to virtually mirror my own – we both had struggled silently for years, we both had ended up in hospital because our bodies had taken the brunt of the strain, and we both had finally decided we had to 'come out'. Vicky, of course, was far better known than I and paid a heavy price in terms of her international music ministry, which was particularly strong amongst American evangelicals.

I have often wondered if the churches that banned her music have ever reflected how bizarre their decision must appear to God. One minute they were using her songs to lead thousands into God's presence, provide healing and enabling people to worship – the next minute they believed it was all ungodly. She had been the same person writing it, performing it, leading it – but now it was 'tainted'. Personally, I have always found her music some of the most healing and authentic that I've ever come across, and it has been my preferred worship music to listen recently to as it's so heartfelt.

---

[1] Available in her moving autobiography, *Undivided*.

Later that Saturday evening I found myself speaking on Radio 5 Live, having rung in to offer my own thoughts and experiences about coming out as a gay evangelical. The next day I was down to preach – for the first time in nearly eight years– and as it 'just so happened' that that Sunday's text was from Isaiah 56: 'For My house will be called a House of Prayer for *all* the peoples.'

Something was happening. I could feel it. Things were starting to change.

I had always known that one day I would need to re-engage with the Church over this issue – but I knew that I needed to wait for a clear signal as to when. Lizzie had been very wary of me getting involved while we were together, but now I was on my own, things were different. However, quite apart from the timing, I also knew God would have to make it clear *how* I was to go about doing this, given I had had no contact with the national church for nearly ten years.

I re-read Vicky's piece and learnt that she had received some help and support from Ruth Hunt, the CEO of Stonewall. I therefore reasoned that this was as good a place as any to start, and so picked up the phone and tried to track Ruth down. She was on holiday, but despite this she kindly rang me back immediately and we arranged to meet a week or so later.

Within a month I had found myself catapulted into the heart of the Christian LGBT world. I had met all the key movers and shakers, including the Revd Benny Hazlehurst, who I had known from my General Synod days, and who had pioneered a new much-needed ministry, Accepting Evangelicals. Benny was an incredible blessing. He asked if I might consider helping him with his work, which I agreed to and so found myself accompanying him to the November General Synod in London.

Things were happening extremely fast – although unfortunately not on the job front. I had been struggling for some time to find work back in Oxford and was beginning to feel totally abandoned by a God who had made things happen so easily in the past. What's more, my CV was a bit of a 'dog's dinner', and I was getting increasingly angry about the fact that I had paid such a high price for stepping off the career ladder all those years ago when I was on the Archbishops' Council.

And then finally, just when I had given up hope, another 'suddenly' incident happened.

Out of the blue, I was asked if I would consider being the interim Director of Fundraising for the Oxford Radcliffe Hospitals Charitable Funds. I explained I had some major charity commitments that I needed to honour, which they were happy to accommodate. This was just as well as Benny had just asked if I would consider taking over from him as Director of Accepting Evangelicals.

On 31 January 2015 I contacted an old friend, Ruth Gledhill, one of the most respected religious correspondents in the media, and asked if she thought that anyone might be interested in the fact I was taking on the role of Director of Accepting Evangelicals, given that I myself was an openly gay evangelical. It was a Saturday night and I didn't anticipate hearing from her until the next Monday. Within minutes my phone was ringing, and Ruth – rather breathless from having made a quick exit from wherever she was – explained that 'if *she* didn't know I was gay then no-one knew!' She advised me that this was likely to be 'big news', given my past involvement with so many senior evangelicals, and that I really needed to think through how I managed the story.

Together we hatched a plan. I travelled down to London to meet her the following afternoon so that she could record an interview with me. It went live in the early hours of 2 February 2015. Over the following few days I was interviewed, as she had anticipated, by some of the leading newspapers and radio stations from around the world – from the *Sunday Times* to the *Washington Post*. Most couldn't believe that a senior evangelical linked to the Archbishops had 'come out' and was now leading an organisation that believed it was possible to be both gay and evangelical.

Within the year I found myself being elected back onto General Synod, and by January 2016 I had launched a campaign to secure an apology to the LGBTI community for the pain and hurt caused by the Church of England, which the Archbishop of Canterbury personally gave in front of the world's media at the 2016 Primates Meeting. I had managed to get over a hundred senior Anglicans to sign the open letter, which I crafted with two new friends – the Very Revd Dr David Ison, the Dean of St Paul's, and the Very Revd Dr Jeffrey John, Dean of St Albans. It was the start of many such initiatives that I would lead to help work towards the full inclusion for LGBTI people in the Church.

And yes, I did eventually end up living by faith again. After leaving the hospital charity in February 2016, I felt that I was being called yet again to trust God and give all my time to serving Him. I recognised that there was little point fighting this call as it was what I felt I had been born to do – and I knew that somehow God would find a way of supporting me through it. Fortunately, for me, towards the end of 2017 a group of friends came together – under the leadership of the Rt Revd Paul Bayes, Bishop of Liverpool – to create a Foundation that would support me in my work. With their help I now have the basis for a more sustainable income stream thanks to the Ozanne Foundation.

The journey to understanding and accepting who I have been created to be – a Christian woman who longs for a life-long union with another woman – has been a long and painful one. It is not a journey that I would wish on any other LGBTI Christian – young or old.

My overarching desire now is to ensure that we are under no doubt that we are each fearfully and wonderfully made, and that the most important truth we must embrace is that God loves us, unconditionally, just as we are.

Postscript

I believe that our desire for intimacy is at the heart of each and every one of us – it is about our need to know and be known, to love and be loved. Whoever that happens to be with. For some – a rare few who have been given the gift of celibacy – this will be wholly met by a deep intimacy with God; for others – indeed most of us – it will also involve the gift of another human being.

It is what is meant when it is said we are created in His image – we are created to 'JUST LOVE'!

Acknowledgements

It'd be fair to say that I've been carrying this book around with me for years. I've always known that one day I would need to write it, but I also knew that the timing would be critical. So I decided to wait until it became abundantly clear that the time was 'now'.

At the start of 2017 things suddenly started to come together. A close friend, who has walked with me through some of my most challenging days - Bishop James Jones KBE – urged me to start writing, assuring me that if I 'just started' then the rest would follow.

A few months later I was offered the most wonderful gift – a couple in Majorca, Rosie and Ken, who had yet to even meet me – asked if I would like to look after their home for them for a few weeks. This meant that I could revisit my past in a sanctuary of beauty and calm.

I came home, and life took over. I needed to secure a publisher and will be forever grateful to David Moloney from Darton, Longman Todd for choosing to get wholeheartedly behind me from the moment we met. He has been a tremendous source of strength, wisdom and encouragement.

In September I looked to crowd source some finance to help me have the time to write. A number of people responded – you know who you are, and I thank you for believing and trusting in me.

And then there are my encouragers – top of the list must be my great friends and neighbours, Ruth McNamara and Jonathan Williams. I can truly say they are the best neighbours in the world! Together we have forged a little

Acknowledgements

community, making our neighbourhood a real place of home.

No book would be of any good without some critical friends who are prepared to give their feedback in a loving and yet insightful manner. David Ison, Colin Blakely and Erika Baker – this book is all the stronger for your thoughts, comments and questions, thank you.

There are also those who have contributed so personally to the book's production. I could think of no one more fitting to write the Foreword than the wonderful and courageous Benny Hazlehurst, who has brought so much hope to those of us within the 'accepting evangelical' wing of the Church. I am incredibly grateful that despite the immense challenges of living with advanced cancer, Benny has found the strength and grace to share his own journey, which has led to him having such a significant impact on both my and so many others' lives. Our prayers are with him and his family, with thankful hearts for all that he has pioneered.

Another gift has come in the form of the image used on the front cover of this book, which is from a stunning painting entitled 'By Your Side' by Lucy Ash of which I am now the proud owner. She has very kindly given me permission to use this image both here and in the logo of my Foundation.

But then of course there are the people who helped create the subject of this story – that is, me. My family and friends – both old and new. Those with whom I am in touch, and those with whom I have lost touch. To you all I say a heartfelt thank you. You have made me the woman that I am, and despite the painful path I've had to tread, I'm grateful for the privilege of knowing you all.

Finally, there is the one who has walked with me every step of the way. The one who has been by my side through every darkest hour and every mountain top experience. The source of all my 'suddenly's'. You have called me by my name and breathed life into my inner heart. You know who You are! My prayer is that all who read this book will come to know You too.

For your name is Love. JUST LOVE.

Amazing Love

Theology for Understanding Discipleship, Sexuality and Mission

Andrew Davison

Amazing Love brings together the wisdom and insight of leading Christian theologians to offer a clear and positive case for the affirmation of gay, lesbian, and bisexual relationships within the Church, as a part of its mission and as an integral part of Christian discipleship for the whole of our lives.

In short, accessible chapters, Andrew Davison (Starbridge Lecturer in Theology and Natural Sciences at the University of Cambridge) explores issues of sexuality in relation to Being Followers of Jesus, Being Human, Being Biblical, Being Part of the Story, Being in Love, and Being Missional.

Price: £8.99
ISBN: 978 0 232 53265 4

Order from www.dltbooks.com or contact
Norwich Books and Music at
orders@norwichbooksandmusic.com
or on 01603 785925

Journeys in Grace and Truth

Revisiting Scripture and Sexuality

Edited by Jayne Ozanne

Is it possible to hold a positive view of same-sex relationships while being a biblically rooted evangelical? These writers believe so.

In this timely collection of essays the Church is urged to listen closely to the experience of leading Anglican Evangelicals who have travelled a path to become affirming of LGBTI Christians in same-sex relationships.

The book includes contributions from Rt Revd Paul Bayes, Bishop of Liverpool, Rt Revd Colin Fletcher, Bishop of Dorchester and the Dean of St Paul's, Very Revd Dr David Ison. It is warmly commended by many, including the Bishop of Gloucester, the Bishop of Manchester, and the Bishop of St Edmundsbury and Ispwich.

Price: £9.99
ISBN: 978 0 993 29424 2

To find out more,
please visit
www.journeysingraceandtruth.com

Our Witness

The Unheard Stories of LGBT+ Christians

Edited by Brandan Robertson

In *Our Witness*, Brandan Robertson has collected the powerful testimonies and experiences of LGBT+ Christians living in active and influential faith today. Some have faced rejection and marginalisation from parts of the Church; some have found fulfilment and blessing through reconciliation 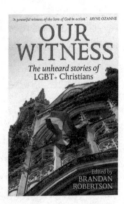 of their faith and their sexuality within the Church; and some bear witness to the great and fruitful revival that the Holy Spirit is bringing about through the lives of the LGBT+ Christian community.

These are stories of faith, hope, love and life, and testimony to a wonderful new work of God in our world today. This unique DLT edition includes a number of stories of LGBT+ Christians from the UK and Ireland.

Price: £12.99
ISBN: 978 0 232 53325 5

Order from www.dltbooks.com or contact
Norwich Books and Music at
orders@norwichbooksandmusic.com
or on 01603 785925